MW00654466

The Way of Discipleship

The Way of Discipleship
Women, Men, and Today's Call to Mission

Anthony J. Gittins, CSSp

LITURGICAL PRESS
Collegeville, Minnesota

www.litpress.org

1   2   3   4   5   6   7   8   9

Library of Congress Cataloging-in-Publication Data

Names: Gittins, Anthony J., 1943– author.
Title: The way of discipleship : women, men, and today's call to mission / Anthony J. Gittins.
Description: Collegeville, Minnesota : Liturgical Press, 2016.
Identifiers: LCCN 2016007163 (print) | LCCN 2016015433 (ebook) | ISBN 9780814647158 (pbk.) | ISBN 9780814647394 (ebook)
Subjects: LCSH: Spiritual formation—Catholic Church. | Christian life—Catholic authors. | Spiritual life—Catholic Church. | Bible. Gospels—Criticism, interpretation, etc.
Classification: LCC BX2350.3 .G56 2016 (print) | LCC BX2350.3 (ebook) | DDC 248.4/82—dc23
LC record available at https://lccn.loc.gov/2016007163

Dedicated, with love

and deep gratitude,

to my family of origin in Manchester, England:

John Gittins (1914–1968),

Teresa Hartley Gittins (1916–2006)

and sisters and brothers

Joan,

Peter,

Stephen,

Angela,

Martin,

and Julie

"The family,

that dear octopus from whose tentacles

we never quite escape,

nor, in our inmost hearts

ever quite wish to."

—Dodie Smith, *Dear Octopus* (1938)

(Born in Whitefield, Manchester)

Contents

Introduction

Who Is a Disciple?

Many years ago a graduate student from Indonesia knocked on my office door in Chicago. A Muslim woman with a doctorate in Islamic mysticism, she was studying Muslim–Christian relations, and she would turn out to be one of the most gifted and personally integrated people I ever met. On this particular day—our first encounter—she had come with one apparently disarmingly simple question: "Are there any Christian disciples in the world today?" Immediately intrigued, I invited her in and asked why the question was significant to her, and she explained. During the course of his life, the prophet Mohammed (570–ca. 632) gathered many disciples around him, and to them he transmitted his revelations and insights. After the prophet's death, however, no more disciples could be added, and when the last of his contemporary disciples died, there would thus be no Muslim disciples left in the world. For Muslims, a disciple is understood to be someone who actually encountered Mohammed and learned directly from him. And this young woman simply wanted to know whether the same criteria applied to the disciples of Jesus.

Very briefly, I explained that, for Christians, anyone at any time could, in principle, become a disciple, whereupon she immediately asked if I would direct her in an independent study of Christian discipleship. She was evidently serious in this request, and I was both intrigued by her original premise and full of expectation that I could gain some further insights into Christian discipleship from

1

her perspective. We sat down there and then and sketched an initial scheme for meetings and readings. Several months later, she wrote a paper—some thirty-five pages in length—on Christian discipleship. It was unquestionably the best-researched, best-written, and most *sympathetic* treatment of the nature of Christian discipleship that I had ever encountered.

It still seems particularly sad to me that even today, some (perhaps many) very committed Christians seem never to have considered that they might be called, personally, to discipleship—simply because nobody ever proposed the idea or encouraged them to do so. Brought up in a community and educated in a church that tended to identify vocation very narrowly as a call to priesthood or religious life, they simply accepted that they were like foot soldiers, rank and file, with no particular distinction or responsibility beyond loyal obedience and quiet faithfulness. "Just a layperson" was a phrase that, sadly, said it all.

Furthermore, there are certainly some women religious who have never considered their own individual call to discipleship and who appear surprised at the suggestion that every vocation is particular and individual. They may have spent decades of dutiful service to God and the community but without focusing on the development of their own personal relationship with God. And more widely among people who may indeed be seriously attracted to the call to discipleship, many look at figures like the rich young man in the New Testament (Mark 10:17-22), and are "shocked" by the "one thing" that overwhelms them—that Jesus looks at them and declares: "go, sell what you have and give the money to the poor . . . and come, follow me." No one has ever helped them to see discipleship—in the New Testament itself, let alone in our contemporary world—as consisting of particular calls to a wide variety of individuals to follow Jesus, but from where they themselves stand and not from where the rich young man stood.

None of us is—or is called to mimic—the rich young man, or Zacchaeus, Mary Magdalene, or Mary of Bethany, and none of us lives in first-century Galilee. And although Christian discipleship is built on a particular foundation—and therefore all manifestations of discipleship share some common features—there is no such thing as a generic discipleship, no "one-size-fits-all" discipleship. Each person is called to respond to the call of Jesus as it touches one in one's own existential circumstances: that is, one's specific geographical, historical, cultural, and personal context. The call to conversion begins wherever we are at a particular point in time and space, and it does not entail the precondition that we literally "sell everything" (Mark 10:21) any more than that we "leave our nets" (Matt 4:20, 22) or "tax booth" (Matt 9:9). Many would-be disciples today have balked at the idea that they must somehow become who they are not. The call of Jesus is not a call for us to become who we are not, but to become profoundly converted by discovering who we really are, who we are called to be, and who we can still become. And since, for Jesus, all disciples are radically equal, no particular example or incarnation of discipleship is in principle superior to any other—something the Twelve would take a long, long time to understand (Mark 10:28-31, 35-44). None of us should have an inferiority complex when we consider our own call to discipleship, but each of us should strive to continuously convert to Jesus himself, and to "the Way"[1] of discipleship.

Pastor, theologian, and disciple Dietrich Bonhoeffer put it like this:

> If Christianity means following Christ, is it not . . . for a small minority, a spiritual élite? . . . Yet surely such an attitude is the exact opposite of the gracious mercy of Jesus Christ, who came to the publicans and sinners, the weak and the poor, the erring and the hopeless. . . . And if we answer the call to discipleship, where will it lead us? What decisions and partings will it demand? To answer this question we shall have to go to him, for only he knows the answer. Only Jesus Christ, who bids us follow him, knows the journey's end. But we do know that it will be a road [a *Way*] of boundless mercy. Discipleship means joy.[2]

The Context for Discipleship

In order to appreciate the nature of discipleship as it applies to each of us today, we really need to place it in its own natural context. Where does it flourish? How does it fit into the great scheme of things? What is its true purpose? And how is it designed to draw us closer to Jesus himself and his own modus operandi? Unless we achieve some clarity in these matters, there will be an abiding danger that discipleship becomes either very self-centered or just a matter of guesswork, and therefore not quite what Jesus had (and has) in mind. This requires not only that we explore and take seriously the wide variety of examples of discipleship in the New Testament, but that we understand what Jesus himself was looking for in disciples—and why. And since Jesus himself explained that he came not to do his own will but the will of the one who sent him (John 6:38; 15:8, 16), we must dig a little deeper and uncover the roots of Jesus' own raison d'être. If indeed he came because he was sent by his *Abba*, what was his mission and how does his invitation to discipleship, then and throughout history, relate to that mission?

The exploration of the nature and purpose of discipleship will take us back to the beginning of time—and even before that. It will require us to contemplate the mystery that is the Trinity itself. But since we simply cannot grasp the ungraspable or understand infinite mystery with our finite minds, we must "stand under" what we cannot understand, be enlightened by the Light itself, and be embraced by the one whom we can never fully embrace. We begin (in part 1) by attempting to bring three concepts—mission, evangelization, and discipleship—into a single frame of reference, to show that discipleship simply cannot be properly understood in isolation from the other two. If we succeed in this, it should leave us all with a profound respect for our own call to discipleship. And then we can look (in part 2) at some examples of discipleship in the New Testament in order to create a profile of discipleship itself, against which we can match our own attempts to be the kinds of disciples Jesus spent his public life seeking, calling, training, and sending.

Discipleship and Faith Formation

This is not intended as a technical or scholarly book, nor is it a book of exegesis that mines the text for precise but sometimes hidden meanings. By no means a biblical scholar, I am a seeker for a more authentic and life-giving following of Jesus. Although there is a degree of exegesis involved, the primary purpose of this book is to assist in some way with adult faith formation. Many of us have not had an opportunity to deepen and develop our faith—specifically our relationship with the Jesus of the gospels and the risen Christ in whom we place our Christian faith and by whose grace we hope it will increase. There are unnecessarily many people who grew up to know their catechism and the religious rules and regulations, but who have not made much progress beyond remembering those rules and the gentle (or perhaps not) Jesus of their own childhood. In these pages, having explored the nature and shape of discipleship in the New Testament, we hope to encounter Jesus through his encounters with others. We then hope to move beyond a simple awareness of some of the dynamics between Jesus and would-be disciples of two thousand years ago, and to apply the lessons to our own contemporary lives in their uniqueness and specificity in terms of our geographical, cultural, and personal circumstances. Without such a reapplication, we risk becoming merely a little better informed perhaps, but no nearer to an ongoing, developing, and sustaining relationship with Jesus, such as would support, animate, and inspire our own daily adult lives.

Faith formation requires the use of our imagination; and faith-sharing evidently requires a community within which to share. Sadly, many of us privatize our faith rather than share it, largely because we are not sure how to share authentically and respectfully without becoming officious or interfering. But the Christian faith is intended to spread by contagion—though never by coercion. Perhaps our reluctance is due to the fact that we are not quite sure who are the appropriate friends or what are the appropriate circumstances in which to share our faith, or how faith formation might best be undertaken. Perhaps even among those we consider to be friends there is not a sufficiently strong basis of mutual trust for us to disclose our own vulnerability, uncertainty, doubts, or "little faith." Obviously we can share faith by the witness of our lives, but sometimes we need to try to put it into words, if only in order to check whether we are as alone as we sometimes feel or whether many other people are also looking for ways to share, just as we are. One of the most saddening realities, for me at least, is to note that many people who actually live in a faith community such as a religious order or congregation, still do not know how, when, or where to share their faith appropriately. Some do, of course; but there are religious sisters, brothers, and clerics who may have lived under the same roof for decades but know less about what sustains or challenges each other's faith than they know of the superficial habits and scandals of "celebrities"—who they are never likely to meet. I believe that there is an urgent need—both in parochial groups of like-minded people and in religious communities—to create opportunities for faith-sharing, whether around the gospel reading for the upcoming Sunday or on a more systematic basis.

Faith Formation Groups

If a half dozen people were to gather as an intentional faith-sharing group, for between half and three quarters of an hour, each with their own copy of the New Testament (but perhaps in several translations) the procedure might be as follows.[3] First, one person would read the gospel passage slowly. Then a short period of silence would follow, during which people visualize and imagine the scene in their own minds, noting the place, the circumstances, the people involved, and the nature of the challenge, rebuke, or encouragement contained in the passage. Then a second person, perhaps with a different translation, would read the same passage again. After another short moment of silence, people would be invited to identify briefly one thing that strikes them, here and now, about the passage.

The first speaker, having finished, would now invite one other specific individual to add another personal reflection or insight that relates to their own current understanding of Jesus' call to faithful discipleship. If that person defers, he or she would then invite another specific individual to share. As each person either speaks or defers, everyone in the group is given an invitation to speak. Then each person who had previously deferred will again be invited and remains free to decline. But when everyone in the group has had an invitation and each person has either spoken or chosen to remain silent, the invitation to speak is again offered to anyone in the group, at which time individuals are free to speak a second time.

But faith-sharing is not a discussion, much less an argument. Each person's contribution stands alone. There is no competitiveness and no attempt at persuasion or changing another person's mind. At the end of an allotted time, the passage may be read for a third time. After another moment of silence, the faith-sharing is concluded. People have shared their own faith and heard other people sharing theirs. Everyone should be enlightened or edified, no one should feel manipulated or browbeaten. And some having now thought of things previously unconsidered, might continue the process by consulting the work of biblical scholars or simply pondering these things in their hearts and hoping to grow in wisdom and grace.

PART I

THEOLOGY, MISSION, AND CHRISTIAN DISCIPLESHIP

1

Mission
Discerning God's Grand Design

Mission: God's Eternal Activity

The word "mission" is often difficult to pin down. It has been and can be applied to a great variety of subjects—from the "mission" of a multinational corporation or that of a covert operation by US Marines or US Special Forces to the "mission" of the church or the "mission" undertaken by missionary communities. Its use is certainly not limited to a theological context. Today, when so many corporations—from McDonald's or Microsoft to the military—and even individuals claim to have a mission or a mission statement, the currency has become seriously devalued. To help our understanding of this word in the pages that follow, we can start by saying simply that we are looking to understand its *theological* application: how the word throws some light on God (*theos*). Our starting point is both simple and profound: theologically speaking, the subject of mission is, first and foremost, God. We are talking about *God's* mission, long before we begin to talk about the *church's* mission or the mission of any ecclesial institution—and certainly long before we presume to talk personally about "my mission." The Latin phrase for God's mission is *missio Dei*: "the (eternal) mission of God." And that is where our reflections will begin. However, we immediately encounter a problem. How can we possibly say anything enlightening about God? God is eternal and a mystery—and mystery, by definition, is incomprehensible.

The Language of Analogy

The fact that God is mystery has certainly not prevented people from writing innumerable words in the attempt to say something comprehensible about God. But a moment's reflection should remind us that although we imagine that it makes perfect sense to say declaratively, "God is truth/beauty/love," and so on, we don't fully comprehend what we are saying. Whatever we know or learn about truth, love, or beauty is obviously limited by our own personal limitations and finiteness. But God is without any limits at all; God is infinite. So when I say "God is love," what I am really saying, implicitly, is something like this: "God is what I *experience* love to be, or what I *understand*, *imagine*, or *believe* love to be—except that God's love is so much greater than that! In fact, it is so much greater than what I know or even imagine as to be utterly different from anything I actually do know or imagine." Saint John simply says that "God *is* love"; and since God is utterly beyond my comprehension, so is the quality of God's love. God's love is inseparable from God's self.

The consequence of the limitations of experience and language is that we must acknowledge that all theological language is no more than an approximation. So God may be somewhat *like* my own poor understanding of mercy, justice, or compassion, but God is so much more as to be *qualitatively* different from my limited perspective. To say "God is like," rather than "God is," is to be transported into the realm of analogy, metaphor, and simile. So can we create some useful *analogies* that would help us to imagine the truly unimaginable God? Can we, specifically, probe more deeply into what God's mission, the *missio Dei* might entail? Fortunately, the answer is a distinctly positive one.

Saint Bonaventure attempted to describe God's activity as *bonum diffusivum sui*, which we might translate as "self-diffusive goodness." Of critical importance, however, this word "diffusive" has a dynamic quality. For example, imagine waking one winter's morning to see the ground covered with snow: the snow is "diffused" right across the countryside. However, this is only part of a dynamic meteorological event—namely, the snowstorm that preceded and caused this widespread diffusion. When we imagine God's "self-diffusive goodness," then, we need to inject into our image the dynamic element: God is the *active agent* causing divine goodness to fill creation and reach into every hidden place—in a similar way to the nocturnal storm that generated the following morning's still and snow-white landscape.

From St. Bonaventure then, we can take the very simple and basic notion that God's activity, God's mission—the *missio Dei*—is dynamic in nature, not static, but also a continuous, never-ending process rather than a single historic event. God's goodness can be understood (by analogy) as God's eternal, dynamic, and sustaining interaction with the whole of creation. And this never-ending aspect of God's mission will become profoundly important to our own attempts to participate in that mission. Nevertheless, Latin tags or aphorisms are not our usual way of thinking or imagining, so it is particularly fortunate for us that in recent decades another analogy—and this time one that is intimately familiar to each of us—has been invoked. Like all analogies, it is less than perfect; but better than most, it does offer us some insight into God's mission. It is usually referred to as the "organic analogy," and it is simply a description of breathing. By analogy then, we suggest that God's mission can be understood rather as we might understand or imagine God's breathing.

A God Who Breathes

We can approach and unpack this analogy rather easily by reminding ourselves that breathing consists of two reciprocal movements:

breathing *out* and breathing *in*. From the first moments of life outside the womb until the final moment of death, both of these activities are required to sustain life itself. It would be ridiculous to instruct one person to breathe out and another to breathe in: each activity is essential and both are necessary as a continuous organic process. The cessation of one marks the end of life. If, then, we can visualize God's mission as rather akin to God's breathing (understanding, however, the rather obvious fact that the divine Creator does not have lungs), how will we distinguish and contrast the characteristic functions associated with breathing out and breathing in, and how will we further describe the dynamic organic activity that together they constitute?

God's "breathing out" can be rather aptly imagined as the dynamic activity expressed in the prayer that begins: "Come, Holy Spirit." It continues, asking God to "Send forth your Spirit and they shall be created, and you will renew the face of the earth." The word mission itself derives from the Latin verb "to send," and is thus related to words like "sending forth." We might then visualize God's dynamic, self-diffusive goodness as God's breathing out, by which God continuously sends forth God's own Spirit of creation. Thus, everything that exists owes its existence to God's creative breath, and nothing continues in existence without God's continuous infusion of God's life-giving Spirit: this is one aspect of God's mission—the *missio Dei*.

Then there is the complementary or reciprocal action: the breathing in. How might we visualize this as God's activity? The Hebrew Bible, the Old Testament, is one long story of God's breathing out and subsequent breathing in of all humanity and, indeed, all creation. After God has breathed into existence all creation and sent humanity—"co-missioned," we might say—to fill the earth, exercise responsible stewardship, and maintain the covenant relationship with God, things begin to go terribly wrong. Expulsion from Paradise is followed by fratricide (Cain's killing of Abel), the Flood, the tower of Babel, and the interminable warrings and wanderings that mark the human story. But through it all, God continues to breathe, not only exhaling or breathing out, but "in-spiring" or breathing *in* humanity (and creation), drawing all things together. If we focus on humanity through the ages, then, we can imagine God's breathing-in as God's never-ending act of inviting, gathering, including, reconciling, healing, unifying, restoring, and so on. In other words, the whole saga of creation itself and of salvation history unfolds through God's creative and sustaining breath, the *ruach* of God, hinted at in the very beginning of the Bible: "The *ruach* of God brooded over the waters," or "hovered"—that is, invigilated, as a hen patiently and persistently broods her eggs until they crack open and the new life bursts out. God's Spirit, then, would be like the mother hen remaining on her clutch of eggs and then with her brood until and after they hatch.

God is in perpetual covenant with all of God's creation—and very explicitly with humanity—and analogies help us visualize the eternal activity of the Trinity, that is, the *missio Dei*. In summary, then, we might say that the word "mission" can serve as a simple, provisional, and easily remembered one-word "job description" for the triunal God acting from all eternity.

Becoming Immersed in the Infinite Mystery of God

We must never forget that God is mystery, and as such is incomprehensible and impenetrable. Nor must we ever forget that ours is a language of metaphor, simile, and analogy only. So we ask whether that is as far as we can go in our understanding of God and God's eternal mission. There are two possible answers, but both amount to a resounding "No!" We can do much better than simply *imagine* God's breathing.

The first answer requires that we remember that when we are talking about or studying matters of God (theology = "study of God"), we are in the realm of faith rather than simple empirical fact. Whenever we attempt to say "God is . . . ," we are asserting or affirming our faith that God exists and that God can in some sense be known. Millions of people in today's secularized world simply do not believe this because they do not find enough empirical evidence, enough brute facts, to support the assertion. But as people of faith, we commit ourselves to the unseen God. Furthermore, we accept the circumstantial evidence of a cloud of witnesses and of what they accept as the revealed word of God written in the Bible or emblazoned on the canvas of the cosmos.

Chicago lies on the edge of Lake Michigan, which is up to 100 miles wide and more than three hundred miles in length. It is possible to stand at a place appropriately called Promontory Point a few miles south of the city, and to look out at this vast lake, which extends across a more-than-two-hundred-degree field of view. So vast is it that it would be literally impossible to drink the lake—to "take it in" or "comprehend" it, so to speak. Having suddenly become aware of that one day many years ago, I returned to my office, contemplating the immensity of the lake and the relative insignificance of myself. But several months later, in high summer I was at the same spot, thinking the same thoughts, when I realized that all around me people were jumping and diving into the lake. Although none of them was able to "take in" Lake Michigan, that immense body was more than able to take in each one of *them*, so that they were immersed and sometimes submerged (but not swallowed up or drowned) within it. It was then that I realized that God can be seen somewhat like the lake and that we are like the swimmers. None of us can, individually or collectively, "take in," "grasp," or "comprehend" the Godhead, but each and all of us can become immersed in God without drowning or being absorbed or engulfed. So the first answer would be simply that we can come to a closer experience of God if only we take the risk, or undertake the adventure, of throwing ourselves into God's unfathomable depths, trusting that God will give us buoyancy and life. When we cannot "understand," we can "stand under"—or in this case take the plunge, in faith, into the immensity of God.

From Analogy to Embodiment

But there is a second (and much, much more satisfying) answer for people of faith. To the question of how best we can come to know God, the answer is quite simple but profound: we do so in and through Jesus. We believe that Jesus is Emmanuel, which means "God is with us"; the Incarnate One of God; God made human, flesh and blood, like each one of us; God who is no longer distant but very close; God come down to earth, down to my level, down to eye level. So the God, Creator and Spirit, whom we cannot comprehend, is "translated" for us into our language and our world and our level of understanding, in the person of Jesus. Jesus is, in other words, the eternal mission of God, but now on earth, among us, one of us—in fact, actually comprehensible. This is the stupendous truth of the incarnation for people of faith. And because of it we can now begin to say that we indeed understand something of the mission of God, because Jesus is it—in the flesh, in human history, in a specific physical and cultural form.

Yet the very night before he dies, it is quite clear that his essential message has not been grasped, when Philip says—astonishingly, given the lateness of the hour—"Lord, show us the Father, and we will be satisfied. And Jesus surely with equal astonishment at Philip's incomprehension, "Have I been with you all this time, Philip, and you still do not know me? Whoever has seen me has seen the Father" (John 14:8-9). And in the course of his final instruction Jesus puts his whole life's work into context: "I have made known to you everything that I have heard from my Father" (John 15:15). But this should not have been news to his disciples; long before, he had intimated and expressed his relationship with the one he called *Abba*, the one whom he identified as having sent or "missioned" him. "My father has been working until now and I am now working" (John 5:17, my translation). "I have come down from heaven, not to do my own will, but the will of [the One] who sent [missioned] me" (John 6:38). "I have not spoken on my own, but the Father who sent me has himself given me a commandment about what to say and what to speak" (John 12:49). He could hardly have been clearer in showing his identification with his *Abba's* will. And of course, when he taught his disciples to pray, he had explicitly told them to pray that "[God's] will [may] be done, / on earth as it is in heaven" (Matt 6:10), indicating that the eternal mission of the Trinity and the mission of Jesus were essentially one, and that it broke through eternity and entered historical time.

Evangelization: The Earthly Ministry of Jesus

The easiest way to distinguish the mission of the eternal Trinity and that of the historical Jesus (although there is no radical break or opposition between them) is to understand that the former exists throughout eternity while the latter unfolded in historic time, in and around Palestine, approximately two thousand years ago. In essence it extended over no more than three years, and many contemporary scholars suggest an even shorter period. But Jesus was now making explicit God's eternal mission for a culturally, religiously, and intellectually specific (and limited) audience, in such a way that ordinary people could now understand—assuming, of course, their attentiveness and willingness to be converted. Matthew's gospel quotes Isaiah and applies his words to the ministry of Jesus: "I will open my mouth to speak in parables; / I will proclaim what has been hidden from the foundation of the world" (Matt 13:35). Nevertheless, many people proved to be hard of hearing and slow to accept—or positively resistant to—his message, including the Twelve on numerous occasions. But sometimes other people— "God-fearers," that is, Gentiles who worshiped the God of Israel— would astonish Jesus himself with their reactions and the depth of their faith in him and his message, putting some of the Twelve to shame and at the same time demonstrating the comprehensibility and accessibility of his message.

If the word "mission" can serve as a kind of shorthand description for the eternal and dynamic activity of the holy Trinity, the very subject of mission, then the word "evangelization" can do similar duty as a one-word "job description" of the historical and dynamic activity of the Incarnate One of God: Jesus of Nazareth. It embraces his whole life's work, and we will explore the details in the next chapter. But before we do that, we ought at least to identify the nature of discipleship and indicate its relationship to mission and evangelization, since discipleship is not only the focus of these pages but must be rooted in something beyond itself—the eternal mission of the Trinity.

Discipleship: Our Life's Commitment

When the ragtag group of disciples finally reconvened after the resurrection, having moved (not for the first time) from astonishment and shock at the sight of the risen Jesus to acceptance of the fact that he would leave them yet again as he ascended to his *Abba*, they would finally grow up rapidly as a result of the Pentecost experience. At that time, as promised, Jesus re-sent the Spirit to be companion, advocate, guide and inspiration to all of them throughout a future without his own physical presence as the historical Jesus.

Jesus had spent his public life tirelessly putting the "zing" into his "evangeli*zing*," his dynamic presentation and incarnation of the Good News. He preached to and healed people as far and wide as his journeys and encounters took him. But in the process he handpicked some to be more intimate companions and confidants. It would soon become apparent that these—whom he called "apostles"—were, albeit slowly and with many mistakes, learning what he wanted of them. In turn many others, both within and beyond the religious tradition of Jesus, demonstrated that they understood the nature of discipleship and some of its cost—and often better than Jesus' inner circle. But one thing was of absolutely paramount importance to Jesus—namely, that he leave behind as many witnesses as possible: people who had absorbed or were gradually absorbing his theology, philosophy, and compassion, and would continue to live it by their words and the witness of their lives. These disciples would become his "witnesses throughout the world" (cf. Acts 1:8) and ensure that his life-giving message of hope and salvation reached beyond the confines of his own ministry, limited as it was by time and geography. Ultimately, they would indeed reach the ends of the earth.

So what, henceforth, would be the specific "mission" of the disciples? First, to have learned from Jesus himself (or later, from those he had taught) and absorbed his inclusive and revolutionary message of love and reconciliation; and second, to go forward in his name, whether in their own neighborhoods or further afield, but always with some of his own urgency and dynamism.

Figure 1

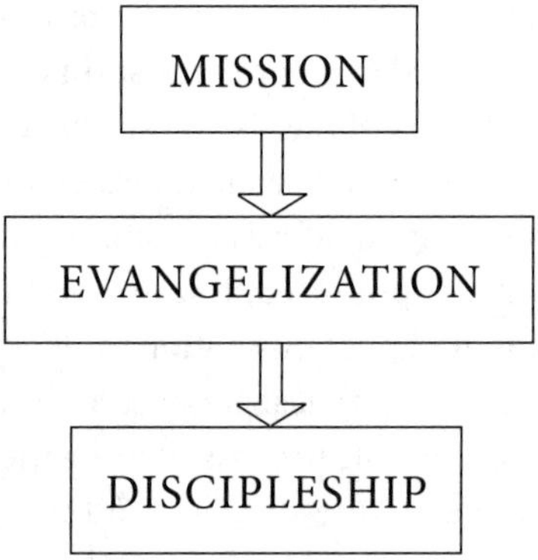

```
┌─────────────────────────┐
│        MISSION          │
└─────────────────────────┘
            ⇩
┌─────────────────────────┐
│     EVANGELIZATION      │
└─────────────────────────┘
            ⇩
┌─────────────────────────┐
│      DISCIPLESHIP       │
└─────────────────────────┘
```

The Integration of Mission, Evangelization, and Discipleship

Having suggested that we can appreciate God's mission if we understand mission itself as a way of describing the eternal and dynamic activity of the Trinity, and that the best way to understand evangelization is as a description of the way Jesus embodies, incarnates, and lives out this mission on earth, we can now describe discipleship as the life's work of all those who are baptized and then confirmed in their baptism as they are both called and sent in the name of Jesus himself. Discipleship, then, is a one-word job description—for disciples, called and sent by Jesus. And since Jesus is totally committed to his *Abba* and the Holy Spirit who sent him, it is easy to see that "mission" and "evangelization" are intimately linked, as a root and its shoot (and indeed its fruit, as it continues to bear fruit age after age). When this happens we can say that when and if each disciple truly strives to do what Jesus did, then each disciple participates in the evangelizing mission of Jesus and, as Jesus says, continues to bear much fruit (see John 15:5). In other words, authentic discipleship is actually a participation in the ministry of Jesus and the mission of the eternal Trinity. In this way, mission, evangelization, and discipleship are intimately linked as God's mission continues on earth, down through the years and centuries, through the commitment of all who have learned from Jesus the Teacher and who go forth in his name rather than on their own recognizance.

What we must now do is return to the mission of Jesus as expressed in his evangelizing ministry, and look more closely at exactly what it entails so that we who presume or desire to be today's disciples will understand what we are called and committed to do. In this way may we avoid the danger of trying to create our own "mission statements" as if we were the initiators and executors of the mission. We are, each and all, *responders* to the initiative of Jesus. We are instruments of the wider mission, the *missio Dei*. As such, today's Christians are called to be authentic disciples of Jesus and live for his kingdom, the realm of God. How, specifically, we undertake this is the topic of the next chapter.

In summary, if we begin with God the Trinity as the subject of "mission," then we need to say that "God's mission has a church" rather than that "the church has the mission." After all, God's missionary activity has existed since the beginning, and the church is only two thousand years old. God managed without the church, for aeons. The church is the *instrument* of God's mission, not its originator or principal. Likewise, religious orders, dioceses, and parishes do not have the mission. They too are instruments. God managed somehow without Benedictines or Dominicans, Jesuits and the rest, for much of human history. And God can manage quite well without them in the future. They are *contingently* necessary, not *absolutely* necessary, and their respective responsibility is to serve and remain faithful to God's mission. But, finally, the mission has each one of us; we do not have the mission. So we do not need to be immortal, and we can pass away in peace when the time comes, if we have tried to be faithful. God, who called each of us, does and will continue to call others to discipleship and faithfulness to the mission.

Chicago's Archbishop Blase Cupich describes the relationship I have attempted to articulate:

> From the very beginning, God has been with us. . . . We have come to know that God is only fully revealed in Jesus, who is God with us to the point that he is like us. But it does not end there. God is so much a part of our lives that the Father and the Son invite us to join in their work of redemption. We do so not as hired hands but as true children, as fully adopted children of God, who through the Spirit of Jesus are able to call God "*Abba*, Father" as Jesus did. . . . God, in effect, placed history in our hands by commissioning us to continue the creation he began. In the great commission to the disciples at the end of Matthew's Gospel . . . , Jesus completes what was foreshadowed in Genesis. There he sends us as disciples to be responsible for how history will unfold, completing his work of creation and redemption.[1]

2

Evangelization
The Form and Content of Jesus' Mission

Evangelization: A Misapplied and Misunderstood Word

The word evangelization is often used in reference to a church program, and sometimes reduced to the act of proclamation or rendered rather bloodlessly as "Good News." None of these will do. In fact, a couple of years ago there were close to one hundred definitions of "evangelization" and "the new evangelization" in print. Evidently these words mean many different things to different individuals and constituencies. But people cannot simply make up their own definitions of things that are already part of our common store of knowledge. In the first place—that is, when the word first appears in the gospels—evangelization is a description of the entirety of the incarnate, embodied mission of Jesus: of his whole life, dedicated to his *Abba* for the sake of God's people. Since Jesus himself "grounds" God's eternal mission on earth in a very specific time, place, and person (himself), and since mission is essentially a dynamic activity, the word evangelization deserves to be understood not simply as a noun but as a verb. It is essentially a "doing" word: the activity of evangeli*zing*.

Since Jesus came to be totally at the disposition of his *Abba* and to carry on the *missio Dei*, the word evangelization (or evangelizing) applies to or describes *everything* Jesus does in his day-to-day activity and throughout his entire ministerial life. For this reason, the word should never be reduced in its applicability—and certainly not to proclamation alone—as if people need to dilute the more technical word (evangelization) in favor of a more accessible one (proclamation). Proclamation is evidently one—but only one—of the many ways Jesus evangelized, but unless we also retrieve the others, we will fail (as, palpably, the first disciples often did) to learn from him and thus to do what he requires of us. Therefore the word itself must be *expanded* so that it embraces the totality of the mission of Jesus.

Jesus *is* the incarnation, the embodiment of the Good News and of the process of "Good-Newsing," we might say. He does not simply talk about love or forgiveness, healing, or gathering: he actually embodies all of these things. He actually loves, he forgives, he heals and gathers, and so much more. And since evangeli*zing* describes his dynamic activity—his breathing out and breathing in, his centrifugal outreach and ingathering—we might reiterate at this point (and because in due course it will be the challenge for each of us) that Jesus puts the "zing" in evangeli*zing*. His whole ministry is marked by his passionate commitment: the zing! Neither is this just a fanciful figure of speech, as we shall have reason to emphasize later. But even speakers of British English, who use "s" instead of "z," can gain a simple but profound insight: they would write "evangeli*sing*," the last four letters of which spell "sing." That is to say, Jesus himself is the *singer*, and his whole ministry is the *song*. He puts lyrics to his ministry so that his whole life is like a psalm or a song in praise of God and in endorsement of God's children. Jesus, then, is both the messenger and the message. This is what evangelizing in the New Testament implies. If those who purport to continue the mission of Jesus through their own discipleship fail to do the same—if they fail to put the "zing" in their evangelizing or to capture the lyrics or to sing of the mission of Jesus—they will betray the very name they preach.

Evangelization: God's Mission Lived Out by Jesus

Evangelization (however spelled) is a single word that can serve as a "job description" of the mission of Jesus, of the whole purpose of the incarnation, of the reason he came to live on earth among us and as one of us. But in order to understand the fullest extension of this word—its outreach and application—we need to use our imagination and visualize the many different components of evangelization that are to be found in the pages of the gospels and in the daily life of Jesus himself. A group of reflective Christians could easily generate twenty or thirty components: from his walking the dusty roads to his preaching; from being fed to feeding others and himself; or from his "deeds of power" to his more relaxed moments with Martha and Mary and Lazarus. But because we cannot easily carry twenty or thirty items in our head at one time, it is fortunate for us that there is a wide agreement among theologians that the total evangelizing activity of Jesus may be gathered under four headings: proclamation, witness, dialogue, and liberation. Together these would constitute *integral evangelization*: they should not be opposed one to another; they do not constitute a hierarchy with proclamation at the top and liberation at the bottom; and we ourselves have no business in our turn to be selective, picking and choosing whichever is most congenial to us as we proceed with our response to the call to discipleship. They do not constitute a multiple-choice selection, and since Jesus did not simply select that which was most convenient or easy, neither must we.

Before exploring each in more detail, it is important to reiterate that these four represent *the way Jesus himself approaches evangelization*, as indeed can be inferred from his own "mission statement" when he declares, "The Spirit of the Lord is upon me, / . . . [and] has sent me to . . . " (Luke 4:18). The catalog or litany he then recites clearly comprises proclamation, witness, dialogue, and liberation, if not in those exact words. But we must note one more component of Jesus' mission, one that might be better understood as its very driving force, the dynamo on which everything else depends: his life of prayer and contemplation and his deep and intimate relationship with his *Abba*. Without such an interior life—as he reminds the apostles in no uncertain terms when they were unable to cure a young boy (Mark 9:18-19, 29)—they, and those of us who follow his Way from generation to generation, will be quite unable to rise to the challenges that pastoral occasions present.

Figure 2

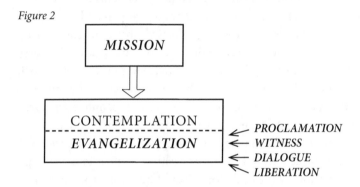

Integral Evangelization (1):
Proclamation, Witness, Dialogue, Liberation

Proclamation and *witness* can be understood as a natural pair, or as two sides of a single coin. Proclamation is typically verbal, systematic, and organized, but people can very easily offer authentic witness without moving their lips at all. Witness is typically nonverbal, spontaneous, and *ad hoc* or responsive to a very particular situation, and people can do it in all kinds of situations. Saint Francis memorably said something to the effect that we should proclaim the Good News always and everywhere, and use words *if necessary*. Evidently, then, words as such are not essential, but proclamation is always necessary, in whatever form it may take. Also, the English word "witness" translates the Greek word, *martur,* which gives us the other English word, martyr. So we can visualize two forms of witness: martyrdom, which costs a life by ending it in a bloody or abrupt and unnatural fashion, and witness, which also persists until the end of life, but in this case death comes in a natural manner.

When applied specifically to Jesus, *dialogue* has sometimes, in Christian history, been deemed an inappropriate word. After all, was not Jesus divine, and thus did he not by that fact know everything and thus have no need of dialogue? Indeed, so the argument goes, if Jesus appeared to be a person of dialogue, he would actually have been pretending. We need to disabuse ourselves of such a view: Jesus, though divine, was also fully human. This is the very profound meaning of the incarnation itself. And as we identify three essential components of dialogue, we can see that each of them does indeed apply to Jesus; he never playacted or engaged in deceit.

First, true dialogue changes both of the participants or interlocutors. Since authentic dialogue assumes that each party is attempting to be Spirit-led rather than just engaged in a zero-sum argument in which one person wins and the other loses, it follows that each is committed to being enlightened by grace rather than fueled by a spirit of argumentativeness. Unwillingness to be led by grace and changed by the Holy Spirit, on the part of any participant, simply demonstrates that whatever happens is not authentic dialogue and that the results are not the mature fruit of true dialogue. The encounters between Jesus and the Syrophoenician (Canaanite) woman (Matt 15:21-28) and the centurion (Matt 8:5-12) are good examples. Having first declared very non-dialogically that he was only sent to the "lost sheep of the house of Israel" and being roundly challenged by the woman, Jesus finishes by exclaiming, "O woman, great is your faith" (Matt 15:21-28); or, as he said to the Roman centurion, "I have not found faith like this in Israel!" (Matt 8:10). The woman's presence, her urgency, and her plea—and the same is true in the centurion's case—changed Jesus' understanding of his own mission, and indeed his interlocutors' understanding of who he is and what he is trying to do. These are signs of true dialogue.

Second, the outcome of any faith-driven dialogue simply cannot be known in advance. Since authentic dialogue consists in a mutual search for God's truth or revelation, each party must remain open to the action of grace. To attempt to control a predetermined agenda is to manipulate rather than yield to the promptings of the Holy Spirit. Therefore, if the interlocutors are two (or more) parties who start from points A, B, C, and so on, about the *only* thing that can be predicted about the outcome of dialogue is that it will be to lead both (or all) parties to a point *other than* A, B, C, and so on. Unless each and every participant in a dialogue is open to being led beyond their own agenda, whatever takes place is not authentic dialogue, however it may publicize itself.

The third characteristic of authentic dialogue can be considered as a structural reality or a fundamentally logical inference: dialogue and hierarchy are incompatible. By no means is this to deny or undermine the place of authentic hierarchy; after all, Jesus himself acts with hierarchical authority, and hierarchical authority is often entirely justified. However, it is to remind us that, for Jesus, and therefore for his followers and disciples, a hierarchy of power (that is, power *over* or domination) is never justified, but only a hierarchy of service (*diakonia*, "service," rather than *archē*, "priority/rule"). Hierarchy itself (whether of power or of service) represents a kind of vertical relationship: one person is in a superior position (super-ordinate) and another in an inferior one (subordinate). By contrast, dialogue represents a horizontal relationship: people are all on the same level. The vertical and the horizontal cannot logically occupy the same space at the same time. There is thus room for a (legitimate) superior to adopt a hierarchical (governing) role in relation to a legitimate inferior or subordinate, but not always or in every instance. Pope Francis is a contemporary example who has refined and polished two perfectly legitimate and compatible roles: that of superior, or structurally hierarchical, and that of equal, or structurally dialogical. But in any given expression of a relationship, each person should be clear whether the exchange is between equals (dialogical) or between leader and led, superior and subordinate, or whatever designation is given to the interaction between two persons of—perhaps temporarily—unequal roles.

As we proceed, then, we will see examples of Jesus in both roles: the hierarchical (when he is teaching and preaching) and the dialogical (when he is seated at table or discussing matters). In the very special case of his encounter with the Syrophoenician woman, it is evident that his stance changes: he seems to start by approaching her in his hierarchical role, but in response to her insistence and persuasiveness becomes much less hierarchical and much more dialogical and respectful. Clearly he has been changed by the encounter—as indeed has she: this is the sweet fruit of true dialogue.

A fourth integral component or pillar of the mission and ministry of Jesus is *liberation*, a word with unfortunately darker connotations in some parts of the church in recent years. But once again it is important to reiterate: when we talk of proclamation, witness, dialogue, and liberation, we are doing so primarily as expressions of the Way of Jesus: the way Jesus embodies or lives out his mission each day. From the time he declares his mission, "The Spirit of the Lord is upon me, . . . [and] has sent me . . ." (Luke 4:18), Jesus is committed to liberation: setting people free from anything that imprisons or binds, demeans, diminishes, or dehumanizes them. To each and every person he encounters, his outreach is focused primarily on restoring their human dignity. As the verses not quoted in Luke's account of the events in the Jerusalem synagogue (Isa 61:3-4) elaborate, restoration is the keynote of the ministry of Jesus. People who are broken down, brokenhearted or broken in spirit or body—all are offered some form of restoration to the humanity of which deteriorating health, bad theology, and the judgment of others have stripped them. Jesus will identify and condemn the bad theology that interprets sickness in mind or body as God's judgment, and he will excoriate those who pile heavier burdens on people already overwhelmed, marginalized, and judged.

When certain forms of proclamation (that is, proselytization: the threat or use of force or fear) or liberation (that is, ideological or Marxist) are opposed by the church, they are not the same thing as the proclamation (never enforced or employed as a form of terrorism) or liberation (always enhancing human dignity and never ideological) as employed by Jesus. Our first responsibility when exploring the four constituents of integral evangelization is to do so with Jesus as their subject, and to identify them as the way he proceeds to carry out the mission of his *Abba* and his Spirit. But there is another way we can identify the mission and ministry of Jesus, and this is by seeing it under four rather different headings.

Figure 3

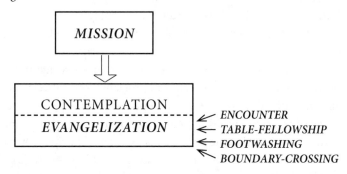

Integral Evangelization (2): Encounter, Table-Fellowship, Footwashing, Boundary-Crossing

Whoever attempts to systematize or interpret the ministry of Jesus inevitably does so by approaching his entire ministry as portrayed throughout all four gospels (and to some degree in other New Testament writings) and then imposing some kind of grid or interpretive device. Every interpretation is a way of reorganizing a corpus of material. Therefore we should not immediately think of proclamation, witness, dialogue, and liberation as explicit markers of the ministry of Jesus, as if these four were somehow written in stone, much less as four distinct programs. In the first place, his ministry was far from mechanical, rigid, or even programmatic (if that word evokes organized programs and entirely rational procedures). Rather than following a fixed schedule, the ministry of Jesus evolved along the lines of a discovery procedure: he set out each day looking to respond to the varied needs of a wide range of people. He was far less program-driven that he was people-oriented. But he was also as responsive to the movement and inspiration of the Holy Spirit as he was to the needs of particular people, and frequently willing to change his mind or his plans according to the eventualities of each day. All of which is to say that in trying to understand the mission of Jesus, we can apply a number of different hermeneutical keys or interpretive lenses. The four mentioned already—proclamation, witness, dialogue, and liberation—may well strike some people as rather too abstract or cerebral. Such people may respond better to more concrete or more familiar images. With that in mind, I offer another set of four essential or comprehensive components of the ministry of Jesus that many people may find more accessible or resonant with their own daily lives. They are encounter, table-fellowship, footwashing, and boundary-crossing.

The first and very simple way to track the intent and ministry of Jesus is by looking at how he proceeds on an average day (if there were such a thing), and what kind or range of people he meets. For his is a ministry, par excellence, of *encounter*. Auschwitz survivor and psychotherapist Viktor Frankl observed wisely: "To love, you must encounter." On reflection, this is patently obvious: we cannot love people in the abstract or in general; we must encounter specific persons, because there simply is no such thing as a person or people "in the abstract" or "in general." There are only particular, individual persons, for God does not make generic. Therefore, the only way to love a real person is by first encountering that person. And this, of course, is precisely what Jesus does each and every day. He goes out of his way to meet, to encounter the kinds of people—alone or in groups—that many people would carefully avoid or encounter in no more than a peremptory or conventional way. When we look at the range of people Jesus encounters—and at the nature of the en-counters—not only do we begin to understand the quality of his interactions and the reality of his love, but we also realize how very far short of his example we fall. So each of us may gauge the distance between ourselves and Jesus—and between his example and our own—by looking at who we actually do encounter, whom we seek out or carefully avoid, and the quality of each of our encounters. The quality can be measured by our attentive listening, our availability or flexibility, our forbearance and tolerance, and our willingness—not simply to provide some token of our cold "charity" or of our conditional response, but to dare to ask other person to identify what he or she really needs.

This is how Jesus deepens his encounter with the blind beggar, Bartimaeus: "What do you want me to do for you?" he asks (Mark 10:51). It is of course much easier to tell other people what we are willing to do for them than to ask what they need. We do good things for and to other people, but far too often it is on our own terms rather than theirs; we remain in control of the interaction. But compare this to the example of Jesus. It would be idle for us or anyone else to claim to love "the poor." Jesus does not love "the poor" but individual persons, one at a time. So the test for those of us to make such grandiose claims is simply to ask ourselves to call to mind their names and faces. Unless we can do that, we do not love real people, however much we may espouse an idea or ideal. And until we take the risk, put ourselves at their disposal, and ask (as Jesus does), "What do you want me to do for you?" we still have a long, long way to go.

It has been said that perhaps the main reason Jesus gets killed is because of his practice of radical *table-fellowship*. He eats with all the *wrong* people in all the *wrong* places at all the *wrong* times. His is a practice of inclusive table-fellowship, in a culture with so many rules and regulations governing and restricting when, where, and with whom one can, or cannot share food. "He eats with tax-collectors and sinners" is the familiar criticism of the one who breaks the rules: and he looks his accusers in the eye, acknowledges that he does indeed include the excluded, and challenges them to do precisely the same. There are three things we might consider at this point: the nature of Jesus' table-fellowship; a comparison between Jesus and ourselves in this matter; and the implications for eucharistic table-fellowship.

Of all the gospels, the Gospel of Luke especially emphasizes the table-fellowship of Jesus, as a splendid little book by Robert Karris highlights.[1] The author shows that most of the time Jesus is found either at table eating, moving from the table after having eaten, or moving table-wards with a view to another meal. Years ago Gerry Brown, former governor of California and subsequent mayor of the city of Oakland, maintained that his current position was much more congenial than had been his tenure as governor, because he was now much closer to the ordinary people. "Start around the table" was his advice to anyone who wanted to make a difference in society. That is very sound theology too, and it could well be the advice Jesus would give his own followers. Strategic use of tables can serve to include, exclude, rearrange, and stratify people: high tables, low tables, circular tables, and rectangular tables, boardroom tables and dining room tables, and more—each one serves a social function, and each can be a way of codifying social relations, whether by separating oneself from or coming closer to other people. For Jesus, table-fellowship was always a way for him to forge relationships of inclusion and to test or erode boundaries of privilege.

Our second consideration would be to look carefully at our own practices of table-fellowship. With whom do we eat, and whom do we avoid? Whom do we invite to our table, and to whose table do we aspire to be invited? With whom would we never think of eating, and with whom would we hope never to eat? And what happened to the family dining table that used to be at the heart of every family and around which the family would gather, almost religiously, at least for Sunday dinner? These days, such family tables are rare, replaced by countertops or dinner trays, or reserved only for special guests and special dinners. Explicitly and implicitly, our choices and aspirations in respect of tables and table companions very quickly identify our habits, our preferences and our prejudices. And as we reflect in this way, again the gap between our practices and those of Jesus seems to get wider and wider: we are so far from what he exemplifies and what he asks of us.

The third point for consideration would be to look at our churches and our eucharistic practices in comparison with those of Jesus. He practiced inclusive table-fellowship (scandalously), while our current eucharistic practice is palpably exclusive (also scandalously). The flyleaf of our hymnals states very clearly that certain people—to our great regret, of course—are not welcome at the eucharistic table because they do not meet our criteria. The scandal that exposes our legalism and judgmentalism is apparent at every eucharistic table and almost every eucharistic liturgy. In the name of Jesus we state that certain people are "unworthy" in a variety of ways, whereas Jesus deliberately sought out and ate with the very people deemed unworthy by his own religious and cultural tradition and even by his own apostles.

People all over the world since time immemorial have understood that in order to survive as civilized people, we need to eat with two kinds of people: with our friends from time to time, but also, and of equal importance, with our enemies if ever we hope to befriend them at some future date. Eating with enemies is also a way to forestall preemptive strikes on their part, as history shows. During the Cold War especially, Kruschev and Churchill, Mao and Nixon, Reagan and Gorbachov would have ostentatious state dinners—not because they were already friends but in the hopes that one day, before they practiced Mutually Assured Destruction (MAD), they might become so. But still we Catholics maintain that we cannot break bread with other "separated" Christians, despite sharing one Lord, one faith, and one baptism, until we have objective proof of our unity. United by one faith, we are still divided over one Eucharist. The theological fault line runs right through our eucharistic table itself. This is the real scandal today.

The third mark of Jesus' ministry is *footwashing*. Footwashing as such is primarily the duty of a slave, who of course has no choice in the matter. But Jesus revolutionizes the practice by washing his own disciples' feet at the Last Supper. They are understandably astonished and embarrassed at this gesture: Jesus is both the host and their master. Yet he insists that he *must* wash their feet and that they in turn must repeat the gesture, not only for their friends but for everyone, including the "nobodies"—otherwise they cannot be his disciples. From shock to enthusiastic acquiescence, Peter then asks overdramatically to be washed "all over": and yet within hours he will run away and betray Jesus. What Jesus asks of his disciples is not that they become slaves, but that they realize they are his friends: friends, unlike slaves, are not compelled. They do have a choice. But for Jesus, this is not a "free" choice: they are required and expected to choose to wash other people's feet—not only literally but metaphorically too. It does not take much imagination for each of us to measure our own "footwashing" against the example of Jesus—from touching "unclean" people of all kinds, to sitting and eating with Simon the leper or Zacchaeus the tax collector.

We remember Maundy Thursday 2013 when Pope Francis washed the feet not of twelve ordained men (as prescribed by the rules applying to the universal church), but of people who were not ordained, not men, and not even Christians! Many pious souls were scandalized, and they were not satisfied by his explanation that he was only doing what Jesus did and what he commanded. But some people are never satisfied. As bishop, archbishop, and cardinal, Francis had been doing the same in Argentina for years. In recent years he has included more prisoners, transgendered people, and other moral "unworthies" or social "nobodies" as a demonstration of the power of Jesus' initial act of footwashing, leaving a clear challenge for all of us: What is the form our own footwashing takes? Whose feet do we "wash," and whose would we never think to wash? Who washes our feet, and whom do we take for granted: employees of the service industries like transportation, catering, or hotel maintenance? Whose feet should we be washing if we hope to be honest disciples of Jesus?

Finally, the ministry of Jesus is marked by his *boundary-crossing* outreach. Boundaries or margins serve a triple purpose: they are points of exclusion, encounter, or connection. The public ministry of Jesus did not take him far from home (the flight into Egypt would have been by far his longest journey, but that was in his infancy); and his normal mode of travel was on foot or occasionally on a donkey. Nevertheless, he consistently encountered boundaries that he negotiated and frequently succeeded in crossing: boundaries of exclusion and privilege, political and economic power, social and gender exclusion, moral distinction, authoritarianism, religious contamination, and purity. Many of the boundaries served a strictly exclusionary purpose, but in challenging rules and practices that excluded rather than included certain people, Jesus asserted that they were unjustified and a travesty of the will of God.

Our own boundaries can be found at or just beyond our fingertips, always at the edge of our comfort zone. We can reach out, take a risk, and encounter and connect—or we can zealously guard our own zone of comfort and privilege, thereby excluding others or refusing to acknowledge them. Jesus negotiates boundaries as challenges to be faced, and his whole life is spent in standing on the edge or boundary between insiders and outsider, trying to draw them together and indeed putting his life on the boundary in order to erase it and become a bridge, as the letter to the Ephesians says so explicitly and beautifully. This is the measure that will be used to measure our own discipleship. "But now in Christ Jesus you who once were far off have been brought near by the blood of Christ. For he is our peace; in his flesh he has made both groups into one and has broken down the dividing wall, that is, the hostility between us" (Eph 2:13-14). So how do we shape up in our own boundary-crossing ministry? Where are the boundaries in our lives, and who populates them? How do we treat people at the boundaries or margins of society, and do we even go out of our way to notice and humanize them, or simply avoid them as often as possible? Do we think of "the homeless," "the poor," or "the foreigner"—or dare we get close enough to look them in the eye and thereby to humanize them as a homeless woman named Sue, a poor child named Emma, or an elderly foreign man named Yusef? How would we measure the distance between the boundary-crossing ministry of Jesus and our own response?

Personal and Communal Applications

Having now taken the word "evangelization," identified Jesus as its primary subject and his entire ministry as its focus, and named its constituent components in two different ways (as proclamation, witness, dialogue, and liberation—and alternatively as encounter, table-fellowship, footwashing, and boundary-crossing), we are ready to face the significant challenge of identifying how we ourselves, as disciples of Jesus, are called to live our lives by following his example and his Way.

But there are two critically important features of discipleship to be considered. First, discipleship is stimulated by a personal and intimate call to each individual; but second, it is also a call to every individual to operate as part of a believing community. Called by name and individually, we are not, however, called to live as individualists, "lone rangers" or loners. Christian discipleship must be lived by individuals in the context of, and as part of communities of faith, whether family, parish, religious community, or a combination of several of these. Consequently, every individual disciple has a double duty: to identify personal responsibilities and to discover how to contribute to the building up of the Christian community (*koinonia*).

In the first instance, then, each of us can examine our personal response to the call of Jesus, according to the example of Jesus himself. How, in my life, can I claim to proclaim, witness, dialogue, and liberate? Indeed, have I ever given much thought to the way I try to live the discipleship I would like to claim? Many Christians have tended to leave proclamation to the "professional" missionaries or preachers, yet it has been a half century since Vatican II reminded us that all the baptized are part of the people of God, sharing a common priesthood and a common call to ministry in its various forms. Pope Francis has reminded us—and with appropriate repetition and emphasis—in *The Joy of the Gospel*, that we are, each and all, called to be "missionary disciples."[2] "The church is herself a missionary disciple" (40). We are all missionary disciples. "In all the baptized, from first to last, the sanctifying power of the Spirit is at work, impelling us to evangelization" (119). "All the members of the people of God have become missionary disciples. The new evangelization calls for personal involvement on the part of each of the baptized. Every Christian is a missionary to the extent that he or she has encountered the love of God in Christ Jesus; we no longer say that we are 'disciples' and 'missionaries,' but rather that we are always 'missionary disciples'" (120).

Unless the components of evangelization (however we choose to name them) are integrated, they will become disintegrated and fail to be the public sign of the fact that disciples of Jesus are still active in the world. Nevertheless, each of us may find, as we examine ourselves in relation to the four components identified here, to be stronger in one than on another, and we may even have overlooked one or other of the four. The challenge for each of us then, is to reflect on how our lived discipleship may better integrate its various components. But we have a second task, since we do not stand alone but constitute part of the *koinonia*, or community of the faithful: we must identify how we collaborate with others by sharing our time and talents in such a way that together, as a community of faith, we account corporately for all four components of evangelization. This is where we can legitimately contribute to the broader community by offering our greatest strength—table-fellowship, perhaps—while encouraging others to offer their own gifts of proclamation, witness, or dialogue. In this way, as communities, we commit ourselves to doing what Jesus was doing and modeling for us, and what he commissioned us to continue doing in his name.

Having now identified evangelization as the entire ministry of Jesus in and around the Galilee some two thousand years ago, we have also specified integral evangelization as the integration of the various component parts of this ministry. Jesus carried out this ministry in union with and in loyalty to his *Abba* who, he explained, had been working from all eternity and was still working. But now Jesus was continuing this eternal mission in a very palpable, down-to-earth way, so that it was now visibly grounded and being done "on earth, as it is in heaven." We can therefore understand discipleship as the work and ministry of those whom Jesus evangelized and called, first to learn from him (as apprentices), and then to go in his name to continue his mission beyond the places he himself visited. We have also noted that discipleship is both a call that is radically inclusive of everyone, but it is also a call to collaboration, to acting in solidarity, and to complementing each other's gifts.

We can now begin to explore the nature of Christian discipleship in the New Testament, so as to build up a composite picture that will act as an example and a challenge to our own response to the call in our own lives. First we will look explicitly at how Jesus understands discipleship and at what he is looking for in those people he calls. Then we will look at a number of specific New Testament passages in order to learn more about the nature and purpose of the call, so that we may apply that learning to our own, very different, lives.

3

Discipleship
Following the Way of Jesus

As we begin to consider discipleship itself, we must relate it first to God's eternal mission and the mission of Jesus, and then we must explore how Jesus presents discipleship and its constituent parts in such a way that we can understand it and try to live it ourselves. Having done that, we will look at how Jesus was in significant ways different from the rabbis of his time. And finally in this chapter we will note one critically important feature of Jewish self-understanding, and see how Jesus exploits this in his own evangelizing mission: listening and hearing.

Mission, Incarnation, and Discipleship

We began with the assertion in chapter 1 that in a Christian theological context "mission" is a word that applies primarily to God as its subject. Mission is nothing less than the eternal activity of the Trinity, expressed in human terms—inadequately, yet also helpfully—as analogous to God's breathing in and out. We also emphasized that since God is mystery, all our language and all our attempts to grasp or "comprehend" God are quite inadequate. But still we try. However, God has taken the initiative and given us a true revelation about this incomprehensible and eternal mission in the person and activity of Jesus himself: God-with-us. As we noted previously (see chap. 1), he is, literally, God come down among us, brought "down-to-earth," we might say, in such a way that the God we can neither know nor see directly now becomes knowable and visible in the flesh. Jesus makes himself accessible, speaks the language of his countrymen and women, walks their highways and byways, visits their towns and villages, and shows himself to them on a daily basis through an enormous range of encounters and in a wide variety of settings. By the end of his life he has made an indelible impression on people of many different stripes and persuasions—some of whom, from historians to chroniclers and from followers to opponents, circulated stories about him and later committed many of these stories to writing. We now have a composite—but evidently incomplete[1]—picture of who Jesus was, who he claimed to be, how he understood his mission from his *Abba*, and how and why he called people to be his followers, his disciples, with a view to becoming what Pope Francis calls "missionary disciples" (see chap. 2), called to be commissioned and sent.

But discipleship is not something people can simply fashion for themselves, and so there can be no self-taught disciples. Jesus is perfectly clear about the nature and purpose of discipleship: he himself is the initiator, and he looks to potential disciples for their response to his call and initiative. *Disciple* is not a self-defining word and does not identify a totally self-sufficient person, for no disciple is an independent agent. Disciples are interdependent, first in relation to Jesus and then in relation to each other. They form a community, united in faith and mission, if not in a specific locality. The word disciple itself is only half or part of a dyad, the paired term being "teacher." Nor is it a particularly sophisticated term, and it certainly does not indicate an expert in some field. Disciple (Greek: *mathētēs*) simply means "a learner" and its verbal form means "to learn."

"Learn from Me"

Our starting point for an exploration of discipleship is Matthew 11:25-29. He begins by praying, "I thank you, Father, . . . because you have hidden these things from the wise and the intelligent and have revealed them to infants." The language here verges on hyperbole. "I thank you, Father, because you have hidden . . . " is a bit like our saying, "Thank God for giving us a nice day"; the nice day, or in the present instance people's willful ignorance, is not a direct act from the hand of God. But the emphasis is surely on the contrast between "the wise and the intelligent" on the one hand, and the "infants" on the other. The "wise [learned]" here (and recalling that disciple means "learner" rather than "learned," a process rather than an achievement) refers to those who *consider themselves* learned, the self-styled learned rather than people who are truly learned. Since a disciple is a learner—forever in training and committed to ongoing education—the self-styled "learned" with nothing more to learn, simply exclude themselves from discipleship. By contrast, those identified by another as "infants" are those who, according to conventional definition and understanding still have a lot to learn. In other words, all those who acknowledge in principle that they still have a lot to learn and consequently seek instruction from Jesus the teacher can qualify as disciples. The Twelve certainly have a great deal to learn, though some of them demonstrate the arrogance of ignorance, which is why Jesus sometimes addresses them rather pointedly as "my little children," precisely to remind them that they still have a great deal to learn. Discipleship itself is a lifelong learning process.[2]

A few verses later, Jesus is even more explicit about what he is looking for in a disciple. He says unequivocally, "learn from me" (Matt 11:29). Here we make an important distinction between learning *about* and learning *from*. Learning *about* someone or something is referred to as academic learning or "outer" learning. It is a perfectly valid form of learning, and particularly applicable to the graduate student who undertakes research and reading about a particular topic. To become a astrophysicist or theoretical physicist, it is not necessary or possible to visit distant planets or undertake direct experimentation on natural phenomena. Both employ mathematics and use abstractions and models to explain and predict. The knowledge generated by such means is perfectly respectable, but academic in nature: it teaches us *about* external reality. By contrast, learning *from*—as Jesus requires ("learn from me")—entails direct contact and interaction with one's teacher. Learning *about* Jesus is surely a worthy enterprise, but that alone will not make people into disciples. In fact the technical words for learning *about* Jesus, or God, are "Christology" and "theology." Such learning is "outer" or academic in nature. So what does *inner* learning look like? It is often called "apprentice" learning because it demands that the learner and the teacher are actually present to each other and in relationship. We think of Jesus as a carpenter because he was also "the son of a carpenter." But he became a carpenter himself, one supposes, not by studying books in isolation, but by being constantly with Joseph as he was turning a lathe to fashion furniture or finishing a yoke. Apprentice learning such as this will produce blisters, cuts, and painful winces with a misdirected hammer—just as an apprentice who is learning to bake will end up with flour in the face and hair, grease on the fingers and hands, and all manner of things on the apron.

Years ago on a Pacific atoll, I was talking to men who once navigated enormous canoes over trackless seas for up to one hundred days and nights, without compass or sextant, radar or electricity. The world's foremost mariners for centuries, they explained that they would carefully select a young boy of promise, maybe only half a dozen years of age, and sit him next to the master mariner, who taught him—by the apprenticeship method—everything he knew about the sea and the sky, the wind and the weather. For voyage after voyage, the apprentice would sit, watch, listen, and learn. To have responsibility for human cargo, livestock, and foodstuffs, one must be carefully prepared. I asked how long the process took. "Until he is ready to die," was the answer. Nothing less than a lifetime is enough time. It is precisely the same for anyone wishing to accept the invitation to discipleship—a lifelong apprenticeship is the price. Discipleship can be neither self-taught nor achieved in the short term.

Ad Gentes Divinitus, the Decree on the Church's Missionary Activity of Vatican II, puts this whole matter beautifully:

> Those who have received from God the gift of faith in Christ . . . should be admitted with liturgical rites to the catechumenate, which is not merely an exposition of dogmatic truths and norms of morality, but a period of formation in the entire Christian life, *an apprenticeship of suitable duration*, during which the disciples will be joined to Christ their teacher. (14; italics added)[3]

So, says Jesus, "learn from me." Not "learn about me" for this is not an academic exercise or the exposition of dogmatic truths or religious rules, but the cultivation of a lifelong and lifetime relationship, born of encounter. Precisely how disciples, in Jesus' time and today, encounter Jesus is a matter we will discover in due course. But the word "disciple" as a noun ("learner") or a verb ("to make learners/disciples"), is the word Jesus used most often—more than 250 times in the gospels, in fact. How people become disciples is by finding and following the way of Jesus. In fact "the Way" is the term used in the Acts of the Apostles to indicate that the early followers of Jesus saw him and his teaching as "the Way,"[4] and followed his Way rather than a path of their own choosing. As the term "the Way" became more widespread, the word "disciple" tended to fall into disuse or was certainly used less, so that in our day we are not particularly used to the word as one that describes ourselves. We tend to use the word "Christian," which was first used around the year 50 CE when St. Paul came to Antioch. Gradually it replaced both the word "disciple" and the phrase "the Way." It is a pity, since "disciple" speaks particularly about a relationship with a teacher. It is that relationship that we will seek to identify in the following pages and, even more importantly, to identify and foster in our own lives.

Jesus and the Rabbis

In the gospel accounts, Jesus is addressed in a number of ways: rabbi, *rabboni*, lord, teacher or master. People who call him "teacher" or "master" are indicating, at least implicitly, that they acknowledge the dyadic relationship that exists between teacher-and-disciple or master-and-learner, sometimes explicitly identifying themselves as his disciples or learners. *Rabboni* is a diminutive or intimate form of "rabbi" used, for example, by Mary Magdalene when she recognizes the voice of Jesus after the resurrection (John 20:16); Bartimaeus shows the same intimacy when he uses the same Greek word while asking for the restoration of his sight. English translations, however, render this as "Lord" (KJB), "master" (Amplified), "rabbi" (NIV), "my teacher, or *rabboni* (NAB/Rheims), or "my teacher" (NRSV). The apparently simple question, "Was Jesus a rabbi?" is not amenable to as easy an answer for a variety of reasons that require the kind of subtle scholarship that is beyond the scope of this book.[5] Rather, we will consider some basic facts and their implications. According to tradition, the fact that Jesus was a young man ("not yet fifty years old," John 8:57), unmarried, and not formally trained made it highly unlikely that he was a rabbi in the sense that word would gradually assume. That he was accompanied by such a large group of disciples, few if any of whom were literate or formally educated, meant that it is virtually impossible that he could have taught them in a way the respected Pharisee rabbis would have approved. True, he was a devout, synagogue-attending Jew who sometimes preached or expounded Torah by invitation; it is also true that he had sufficient learning for people to wonder where and how he could have accumulated it (Mark 6:2). But he was also something of a mystery, refusing to allow his followers to accept the title "rabbi" (Matt 23:8) and calling anyone who took titles themselves hypocrites (Matt 23:13-37).

Of particular interest to us however, is the fact that, "rabbi" or not, Jesus was indeed different from the conventional teachers or rabbis in three ways that are pertinent to our exploration of discipleship. First, as biblical scholar John Meier affirms, "individuals sought out a religious leader or guru; the guru did not peremptorily call individuals to follow him as disciples."[6] John the Baptist certainly did not; but Jesus did. Not only did he call some people explicitly— Peter, John, James, Andrew, Levi, and the rest—but one of the very last things he did was remind them very explicitly of that fact and its significance: "You did not choose me but I chose you. And I appointed you to go and bear fruit, fruit that will last" (John 15:16). Here we have the clearest possible statement that it is Jesus who takes the initiative and calls, and that the purpose of the call is the co-missioning or sending forth to proclaim the Good News.

Second, one of the most sacred duties of the teachers, Pharisees, or rabbis of the time was to receive the Torah respectfully, absorb it wholeheartedly, and transmit it faithfully. Jesus subscribed to each of these tenets, but with a twist. Although he declared that he had not come to modify or change "one letter" or "one stroke of a letter" of the law (Matt 5:18) he declares, in the synagogue one Sabbath, a woman healed of her infirmity and affirms that the Sabbath was made for people such as her and not the other way around. He then calls the synagogue officials hypocrites for complaining (Luke 13:14-16). And he makes statements like this: "You have heard it said . . . But I say to you" (Matt 5:21-22, 38-39). Notwithstanding his respect for tradition, Jesus clearly feels free to inject, when appropriate, what we might call pastoral creativity or sensitivity, making exceptions for the sake of those in need.

The third difference between Jesus and his contemporary teachers is that for him discipleship was radically inclusive: women were not only included but often showed themselves superior to the men in every department—faithfulness, understanding, and commitment to his mission. This was decidedly countercultural in that place and time, where women had a very attenuated legal status and public profile. For Jesus, not only was discipleship radically inclusive, it was also radically equal.

Disciples and Apostles

We should note from the outset that in the New Testament, the word "disciple"—as indeed the word "apostle"—is used (confusingly) both in a narrow, restricted sense and also in a broader, more inclusive sense. In the former sense it applies specifically to those who are called by Jesus, develop a personal relationship with him, and form a community devoted to proclamation of the realm of God. In Luke's gospel, particularly, the twelve disciples are routinely called apostles. However, in the broader sense, "disciple" applies to anyone who shows real faith and trust in Jesus and whose encounter with him produces a conversion to the Way of Jesus. This is why we ourselves can claim to be latter-day disciples of Jesus. Sometimes the word "disciple" applied only to the Twelve (apostles), but at other times to a much more inclusive group: context usually clarifies the intended audience. The word "apostle" literally means "one who is sent," and in that sense virtually everyone who encounters Jesus and strives to follow him is caught up in the mission of Jesus, of which proclaiming the realm of God is an integral part. People are called, not simply to be with Jesus in some safe and cozy relationship, but in order to be sent; and disciples are commissioned as apostles to continue this work. However, in a restricted sense, the word applies to "the twelve apostles." The only two criteria for an "apostle," however, were, first, to have been with Jesus from the beginning and, second, to have been a witness to the resurrection. Clearly Paul—who calls himself an apostle—does not literally fulfill either criterion; but equally clearly, many of the women who followed Jesus certainly did.[7] And Paul seems not to have known of (or perhaps resisted) the restricted sense in which the word apostle was used (1 Cor 15:5, 7). So we have to be careful when we encounter the words "disciple" and "apostle."

The Importance of Hearing

There is one addendum to mention, and it is particularly important because it affords us a most helpful key to understanding the pastoral psychology of Jesus: his emphasis on careful listening and hearing. One thing biblical scholars and commentators remark upon when discussing the Jewishness of Jesus is the importance of the

Shema, the rallying call of every Jew, articulated in Deuteronomy 6:4-9, which Jesus would have known, treasured, and recited faithfully every day:

> Hear [Listen], O Israel: The LORD is our God, the LORD alone. You shall love the LORD your God with all your heart, and with all your soul, and with all your might. Keep these words that I am commanding you today in your heart. Recite them to your children and talk about them when you are at home and when you are away, when you lie down and when you rise. Bind them as a sign on your hand, fix them as an emblem on your forehead, and write them on the doorposts of your house and on your gates.

Clearly this was understood as monumentally important. Behind it lies a conviction that appears to be at the very heart of Jewish self-understanding: that, for this people, one of the primary defining characteristics of human persons is the ability to listen, to hear, to internalize, to reflect, and then to act.

Every human society has striven to define what is quintessentially human, but the Jewish intuition about "having ears" gives us an exceptionally fine tool with which to gauge people's authenticity and their response to Jesus. Jesus himself appeals to this throughout his ministry. His teaching is largely in parables, stories, anecdotes, and such, and he asks little more than that people should pay attention, listen, and then respond appropriately. Some people, of course, are not serious. They may be curious and enjoy a story, but their interest is superficial. One day, after Jesus has told the parable of the Sower, Peter asks—in a typically shallow, arrogant, or simply inappropriate way—"Why do you talk to them in parables?" as if Jesus needs to talk down to *them* in contrast to the way he will talk to his "chosen." But Jesus pricks this Petrine bubble beautifully. He intimates that some people are not really using their ears to listen and internalize, but simply to be entertained. In such cases, his words will go in one ear and out the other. He says, quoting Isaiah,

> "For this people's heart has grown dull,
>> and *their ears are hard of hearing*,
>>> and they have shut their eyes;
>>> so that they might not look with their eyes,
>> and *listen with their ears*,
>>> and understand with their heart and turn—
>>> and I would heal them." (Matt 13:15)

But then Jesus turns and seems to humor Peter, saying,

> But blessed are your eyes, for they see, and *your ears, for they hear*. Truly I tell you, many prophets and righteous people longed to see what you see, but did not see it, and to hear what you hear, but did not hear it. (Matt 13:16-17)

And yet, in the next breath, Jesus skewers Peter's pretentiousness by showing he is perfectly well aware that Peter himself has failed to understand the parable. His next word, addressed not only to "them," but to Peter himself, is simply, "*Hear*" as he rather painstakingly explains the parable (something that should be quite unnecessary) by using the word "hear" five consecutive times to apply to those who receive the seed and apparently "hear" but fail—except in the final instance—to bear fruit. It is a well-made and well-taken lesson that sets the stage for the ministry of Jesus and his repeated emphasis on the necessity for hearing and doing.

One time, a woman in the crowd, wishing to praise the mother of Jesus, shouted out, "Blessed is the womb that bore you and the breasts that nursed you!" A fine, earthy tribute, this. But Jesus responded, surprisingly, "Blessed rather are those who *hear* the word of God and obey it!" (Luke 11:27-28). And on another occasion, Jesus declared,

> Not everyone who says to me, "Lord, Lord," will enter the kingdom of heaven. . . . Everyone then who *hears these words* of mine *and acts* on them will be like a wise man who built his house on rock.

The rain fell, the floods came, and the winds blew and beat on that house, but it did not fall, because it had been founded on rock. And everyone who *hears these words* of mine *and does not act* on them will be like a foolish man who built his house on sand. The rain fell, and the floods came, and the winds blew and beat against that house, and it fell—and great was its fall! (Matt 7:21, 24-27)

Finally, we might recall that when some of John's disciples or followers approached Jesus with a question from the Baptist: "Are you the one who is to come, or are we to wait for another?" Jesus simply said, "Go and tell John what you *hear* and see" (Matt 11:3-4).

I italicized these references to hearing in order to remind us of how crucial it is to any would-be disciple. As we look at examples of Jesus' actual encounter in part 2, we will again have occasion to notice his emphasis on hearing and acting.

4

The Way of Jesus, the Way to Discipleship

Overview

Before we can explore the New Testament accounts of discipleship, it would be helpful if we had some ideas of what to be on the lookout for, since there are significant indicators, here and there, of whether a person has the makings of a true disciple or not.

Consequently, we will identify "the Way" of Jesus; faith and miracles; steps to faith; stages of discipleship; and the subject of "recontextualization" (that is, how we might apply stories from two thousand years ago to our own contemporary lives). Unless we make this final step, all we will have achieved is something of antiquarian interest but not enough to motivate us to a more committed following of Jesus as his latter-day disciples. Only when we have completed that preliminary work will we be ready to examine specific New Testament passages as illustrations of discipleship. But before we look at the themes that relate explicitly to discipleship, there is one other matter that needs to be identified. This one certainly applies to would-be disciples of Jesus but in fact has a much longer pedigree: it goes back to the ancient self-understanding of the Jewish people themselves. It is an attempt to specify what it means to be human, since discipleship is specifically intended for human beings.

Human Beings, Not Angels

There is a broad stratum of Christian spirituality that, in focusing
on our call to holiness, has tried to persuade people that spirituality
is *opposed to* the body or embodiment, and even that we humans
should aspire to becoming like the angels. What we now call "spirituality" used to be more familiar to previous generations as "ascetic
theology," with the emphasis on the ascetic component. But these
emphases are very wide of the mark proposed by Jesus himself. In
the first place, Jesus is, literally, the very *embodiment* of God: God-
made-man or God-become-human; the Incarnate One of God. The
incarnation is one of the central pillars of the Christian faith: God
becomes human in order to show us how to become more fully
human, and thus Godlike. Recall that St. Irenaeus said that the glory
of God is the fully-alive human person. But not everyone is fully
alive, sadly.

The technical name for this theological notion—much more de-
veloped in the Eastern church than the West, and thus relatively
little-known in the West—is *theosis*. The word is sometimes rendered in English as "divinization," which is not, however, a happy
word choice. We are not made to be divine; we are not God. But the
theological idea includes the argument that even if there had been
no fall or original sin, God would nevertheless have come to us as
Jesus, the Incarnate One.[1] So, rather than seeing the incarnation
only as atonement (Jesus somehow compensating for original sin),
we can see it as part of the eternal plan of God. Jesus comes in order
to show us how to live in a fully human way, and not as people who
fail to understand of appreciate their potential. Saint Athanasius
(296–373) said, "He was incarnate that we might be made God."[2]
Saint Irenaeus (ca. 130–ca. 200) put it this way: "God became human
in order that human beings would become God."[3] And St. Maximus
the Confessor (580–662) is widely quoted on the subject. We are
more than animals, and not only "fallen" humanity; we are "re-
deemed," chosen, called, anointed, and sent as people imbued with
the very Spirit of God—hence "divinized."

When the water is mingled with the wine at the offertory in the liturgy, the presider says (too often silently, and sometimes not at all) the following prayer: "Through the mystery of this water and wine may we come to share in the divinity of Christ who humbled himself to share in our humanity." This expresses part of the notion of *theosis* beautifully: we come to share in his divinity! And the Catholic catechism combines quotations from each of these Christian writers, mentioning theosis several times.[4]

So Jesus comes, not to placate an angry God who demands, as the price of satisfaction, the sacrifice of the very life of Jesus. He comes to us in order to encourage us and exemplify for us what it can mean to live up to our potential as human beings. If being fully human is good enough for God (as it is!), we might think that it should be good enough for us. But it has not always seemed so.

Incarnation, or embodiment, does not oppose body and spirit (*pneuma*), because we are in fact "inSpirited" people. But it does oppose spirit and flesh (*sarx*), the latter identified by St. Paul as the shallow, selfish, sinful, greedy, grasping self. That false self is certainly opposed to the true self, the noble, altruistic, generous, self-sacrificing, affirming self that we see exemplified in the life of Jesus.

The letter to the Hebrews is even more explicit. As the Jerusalem Bible puts it, "It was not the angels that [God] took to himself; he took to himself descent from Abraham. It was essential that he should in this way become completely like his brothers [and sisters], so that he could be . . . compassionate and trustworthy" (Heb 2:16-17).

And yet for many Christians there has been a real struggle in a vain attempt to become more like angels than human persons, almost disembodied rather than fully embodied. In fact the history of the word "spirituality" itself—originally coined by St. Jerome (d. 420) to mean "the new life of the Holy Spirit received in Christian baptism"—gradually lost its original meaning in English. It came to mean, first the clergy, then ecclesiastical property, then preposterously, "incorporeality" (*not* having a body), and finally "refinement"

or a mode of social or intellectual sophistication. But any attempt
to repudiate the body is almost sacrilegious in itself. We are made,
in God's image, as human persons, "inSpirited" bodies, or body and
soul. There is no other way to become a true disciple than by living
our humanness to the full, as Jesus did.

"The Way" of Jesus

"The Way of Jesus" and "followers of the Way" were phrases that
identified for the early church the path of discipleship and those
who attempted to follow it. The word itself, "way" or "road" (Greek:
hodos), occurs numerous times in the New Testament, but nowhere
more frequently than in the Gospel of Mark. The evangelist—and
the others use the same designations less frequently—constructs his
narrative around a dominant theme: Jesus is on the road or on "the
Way" to Jerusalem and destiny; nothing will distract him from that
commitment; and would-be disciples will be apprised in no uncertain terms that this is the *only way* for faithful disciples as far as Jesus
is concerned in his own context. (Many people might aspire to be
disciples—then and now—but some always want to do so in their
own "way" and in their own time; this will simply not work). But
as Jesus is *on his way* to Jerusalem, he will deliberately go *out of his
way* to seek and find people who have *lost their way* or are *by the
wayside*, in order to call them back to "the Way" of discipleship.
Stated thus, the occurrence of *the Way* or *the road* becomes much
more noticeable to the reader, and the image of Jesus *on his way*,
and disciples coming to his *Way*, becomes easier to follow as we
work though the gospel narrative. The opponents of Jesus quickly
identify his strategy, saying, "You teach in truth *the way* of God"
(Mark 12:14). But Mark also shows, sadly, that the disciples—and
this is particularly true of the men, the chosen Twelve—are very
resistant to *his* Way, often expecting things to go *their* way, and being
upset when they do not. In truth, they have a lot to learn: they often
act like peevish children.

Jesus, a Miracle-Worker?

Was Jesus a miracle-worker? Is that an appropriate description of his ministry? A moment's thought should remind us that it was just about the last thing Jesus wanted to be identified with. He was not looking to attract "gapers" or people coming to him simply out of curiosity. Nor did he seek what today would be called celebrity status. We know this because of what is referred to by scholars as the "messianic secret." Oddly perhaps, at first sight, when Jesus does perform some work of power, some miracle, he warns the beneficiaries not to tell anyone about it (Matt 8:4; 9:31; 16:20). That is not exactly a realistic hope when lepers are made clean and paralyzed people stand up and walk! The first thing they think of doing is showing themselves to the priests and appearing in public as soon as possible thereafter.

Nevertheless, Jesus strenuously resists becoming some kind of popular celebrity or cheap miracle-worker—of whom there were many, all bogus, to be found. First and foremost, Jesus came looking for faith among a broken and demoralized people. With their history of deportations and slavery, and their current experience of living under the rule of the Roman Empire—a foreign power that taxed them relentlessly and treated them disdainfully—they had lived for centuries on the promises of prophets but with the bitter experience of dwelling in an occupied land and with no signs of the freedom and dignity for which they hoped and prayed. So Jesus took upon himself a dual task: he went about looking for faith among the chosen people, and also sowing seeds of faith and hope where there were few or none. Strictly speaking therefore, he was a "faith healer" (if that title had not been abused and debased): he proclaimed that if people had faith, miracles would happen. Faith makes miracles, he declared; but miracles rarely make faith, as he knew from his own visit to his hometown when, after lionizing him, the people quickly turned on him, tried to throw him off a cliff, and decided that he was out of his mind (Luke 4:30; Mark 3:21). "And he could do no deed of power [miracles] there. . . . And he was amazed at their unbelief" (Mark 6:5-6).

Steps to Faith

If we take an overall or comprehensive view of the New Testament narratives, concentrating on the various encounters between Jesus and numerous individuals and groups, we can begin to see the emergence of a pattern. People may come to faith in a variety of ways, but they may also show very promising early signs, only to fall back into serious doubt—or even denial and betrayal. Some people seem to have solid faith as soon as they appear in the narrative—notably some of the women, who do not always speak but demonstrate their faith through their actions. Generally however, we can track people's approach to faith in Jesus by looking at the ways in which they address him, noting if their mode of address bespeaks growing faith as they come closer to a relationship with Jesus.

We can imagine a scale: at one end would be no, or very faint, indications of faith, while at the other would be demonstrable acts of fervent faith. For example, some people shout the name of Jesus or address him as "master" or "teacher" or "rabbi," leading us to ask ourselves whether they actually believe in him and commit themselves to him, or whether theirs is simply a conventional mode of address. At the other end of the scale, however, we find full-blown faith statements like Thomas's five concise words, "My Lord and my God." Nevertheless, as Jesus himself says, "Not everyone who says to me, 'Lord, Lord,' will enter the kingdom" (Matt 7:21). Actions speak louder than words, and Thomas himself did not come to mature faith without a struggle. It was Thomas who had declared so petulantly, "Unless I see the mark of the nails in his hands, and put my finger in the mark of the nails and my hand in his side, I will not believe" (John 20:25).[5] In a rather different tone, Peter started magnificently with "You are the Messiah, the Son of the living God" (Matt 16:16)—a faith statement if ever there was one. But before long he was cowering before a serving maid, denying Jesus three times, and saying flatly, "I do not know the man" (Matt 26:70-74).

So, we can look at the responses of various people as they encounter Jesus, in order to determine whether they have faith or are coming to faith by degrees. Typically people take two or three—and in the case of the woman at the well—five attempts, before finally identifying Jesus as the one whom they believe and in whom they put their trust (see chap. 12). Some of the women do not say a word but demonstrate their faith very palpably with their silence, while it is another woman—not a man and not one of the Twelve—who makes the most sophisticated faith statement in the whole of the New Testament. It is the much-maligned Martha who affirms, in the high Christology of John's gospel, "Yes, Lord, I believe that you are the Messiah, the Son of God, the one coming into the world" (John 11:27).

How people come to faith—or in some cases, how they fail to do so—can often be gauged by the way they name and identify Jesus. For example (as we will see in chap. 7), Bartimaeus (Mark 10:46-52) identifies Jesus, first as "Jesus, Son of David, have mercy on me," then more urgently, "Son of David, have mercy on me," and finally, "My teacher, let me see again." "Teacher," as we saw, is the term that is paired with "disciple" or "learner," so this indicates that Bartimaeus, in seeing Jesus as the Teacher, also sees himself as Jesus' disciple. But more than that: Bartimaeus says explicitly, "*my* Teacher," which is the phrase Mary of Magdala uses on the day of the resurrection: *Rabboni* (John 20:17). By contrast, the rich man, earlier in the same chapter of Mark (whom we consider in chapter 5), identifies Jesus first, and rather promisingly, as "Good Teacher," but later, and a little more testily as he justifies his own religious observance, addressing Jesus rather less warmly, simply as "Teacher." And sadly, that is literally his last word. He is shocked by what Jesus has to offer, and goes away—goes his own way, the same way as he had come, and not "the Way" of Jesus, the way of discipleship—"grieving, for he had many possessions" (Mark 10:22).

Stages of Discipleship

Being on the lookout for the way different people address Jesus, or indeed approach him wordlessly, we may more readily appreciate the dynamics of discipleship. But there is at least one more thing we can identify, and that is what we might call the stages of discipleship. Again, it is more a matter of looking across the whole panorama of the New Testament, specifically the gospel stories, to see if we can perceive or deduce a pattern. Discipleship does indeed have a shape or form; it is not something vague or evanescent, and when Jesus looks for potential disciples, he does not do so in some random fashion. He is looking for certain qualities and a certain disposition that, frankly, not everyone possesses. But he is not looking for clones, and there is no such thing as a "one-size-fits-all" discipleship. As we look across the full range of gospel stories, it seems that mature discipleship is the result or outcome of a relationship between Jesus and another person that develops in three stages. First, there is call or an encounter; then, there is a disturbance or a displacement; and, finally, there is a sending forth or a "co-missioning." We can examine each of these in turn.

(1) Call or Encounter

The call of the first disciples represents the classic case. In Matthew's account, Jesus is walking by the Sea of Galilee when he sees the brothers Simon and Andrew, calls them without any preamble to follow him, and they, in turn, immediately leave their nets (and presumably family and coworkers) and follow Jesus (see Matt 4:18-20). In Mark's account, the brothers James and John are also called, and, like Simon (Peter) and Andrew, respond immediately—in this case leaving "their father Zebedee in the boat with the hired men" (Mark 1:19-20). A little later, also by Lake Tiberias or the Sea of Galilee, he saw Levi the tax collector, called him to follow, and Levi immediately did exactly that (Mark 2:14). We are very familiar with these stories, of course, and many other similar accounts. The call—in these cases, explicit and personal—results in Jesus and would-be disciples coming face to face for the first time.

But there is another way for Jesus to come face to face with a would-be disciple, and that is simply by an encounter that does not result from an explicit call or personal invitation. The rich man (Mark 10:17) and the woman with the hemorrhages (Mark 5:27), among others, were not explicitly called by Jesus: the former virtually threw himself at Jesus' feet, while the woman crept up behind him and touched his robe. But the encounter between each of these and Jesus represented a turning point in their lives. In other words, whether by explicit call or by encounter, the stage is set for the possibility of becoming a disciple. But it is not automatic or inevitable; it would take a considerable amount of time, with mistakes and backsliding, before Peter, James, and John and the rest of the Twelve would become true disciples—and that would really be only after the transformative experience of Pentecost and the coming of the Holy Spirit. In fact Jesus warned them—much to their surprise—that discipleship was actually impossible for them to accomplish on their own. Discipleship can only happen with God's help and grace (Mark 10:23-45).

We may easily, but quite wrongly, assume that the Twelve are the best examples of discipleship, but as Elizabeth Schüssler Fiorenza aptly observed—as portrayed in the Gospel of Mark—the Twelve are in many ways examples of precisely how *not* to be disciples or how *not* to respond to the call. They make so many mistakes and jump to so many wrong conclusions. In fact, generally speaking, the best examples of discipleship are to be found in the women who populate the gospel accounts—despite the fact that in none of the gospels is any woman actually identified as a disciple (using the feminine form of the word *mathētēs*, "learner": *mathētria*).[6] Matthew's gospel account often covers the embarrassment and the blushes of the Twelve, whereas Mark's tells a rather more human story of these would-be disciples, "warts and all." Compare Matthew's ending of the story of the storm at sea: "When they got into the boat, the wind ceased. And those in the boat worshiped him, saying, 'Truly you are the Son of God'" (Matt 14:32-33). But here is Mark's ending: "Then he got into the boat with them and the wind ceased. And they were utterly astounded, for they did not understand about the loaves, but their hearts were hardened" (Mark 6:51-52). The Jerusalem Bible is even more trenchant at this point: "They were utterly and completely dumbfounded, because they had not seen what the miracle of the loves meant; their minds were closed."

As we will see later, encounter is one of the hallmarks of the mission and ministry of Jesus: it is a major way in which he actually carries out his mission. It is also how he often opens the way to discipleship. But the call does not make the disciple: there is much more to the story; and in many cases, the call (or encounter) serves as a prelude to the second stage of discipleship, the disturbance or displacement.

(2) Disturbance or Displacement

The course of discipleship and the following of Jesus are not without their challenges: true discipleship entails a denial of one's false self, a taking up of life's crosses in their many forms, and a real rather than a notional commitment to Jesus. Bonhoeffer expands on this commitment:

> Discipleship means adherence to Christ. . . . An abstract Christology, a doctrinal system, a general religious knowledge on the subject of grace or on the forgiveness of sins, render discipleship superfluous . . . and are essentially inimical to the whole conception of following Christ. . . . Christianity without the living Christ is inevitably Christianity without discipleship, and Christianity without discipleship is always Christianity without Christ. . . . And a Christianity of that kind is nothing more or less than the end of discipleship. In such a religion there is trust in God, but no following of Christ.[7]

In other words, we need to come to know Jesus intimately (through apprentice knowledge) rather than simply to know about him (through academic knowledge). Many characters and persons in the New Testament account know about Jesus to a greater or lesser extent, but his true disciples—then and now—are those who strive to know him in a personal way and who cultivate a developing relationship with him, something we will certainly explore in greater detail as we proceed. The Muslim woman whose story opened this book was particularly intrigued with this idea. She was impressed with the notion that two millennia after his death, people should still seek and indeed claim to have a personal, developing relationship with the one who was crucified, who rose from the dead, and who lives today as the risen One of Christian faith.

A disturbance or a displacement, in the sense intended here, is some unexpected event or challenge that causes a person to take stock of his or her current circumstances and generate a response, whether positive or negative. A positive response would be indicated by an immediate willingness to follow the initiative presented by Jesus, even though it is neither foreseen nor easy to accept. A negative response would be a patent refusal to listen or respond, or at least an immediate resistance to the Jesus initiative. The rich man (Mark 10:22) "was shocked and went away grieving"—a decidedly negative response, at least initially, but who can say what grace might accomplish later? Another negative reaction would be that shown by Peter when Jesus is explaining the cost of discipleship (Mark 10:22-45) or when Jesus says that he himself must suffer and die: "God forbid," says Peter, resisting the very idea: "This must never happen to you" (Matt 16:22). We will see other reactions and responses. Sufficient at this stage is to invoke sentiment of respected Scripture scholar James D. G. Dunn, who says that there is a disturbing quality about the urgency of Jesus' call: a shaking of the foundations—such that those who want a quiet life are bound to resent and resist it. All of us some of the time, and some of us all of the time, want a quiet life; therefore if Dunn is right, as intuition confirms, all of us will encounter our own personal resistance and even resentment when we feel the disturbing call of Jesus—or the displacement it causes in our ordered and controlled lives.

It might be helpful to recall that the God of Israel, the God of the Hebrew Bible is, in fact, a God who disturbs: a disturbing God. This is not typical of people's understanding of God cross-culturally or down through the ages. In many cultural religious understandings,

God is distant, removed from human contact, and extremely difficult to communicate with: hence the need for and presence of intermediary spirits or prophetic figures. This is the *deus otiosus* (literally, the "lazy god," but meaning the withdrawn god). But the God of Israel is a God of covenant—and of a covenant that was unique in the ancient world. There are plenty of examples of rulers who established a covenant with their people, but such covenants were typically unilateral and threatening, rather than reciprocal or affirming. The ruler would dictate what the people should do in order to avoid punishment (including death) and then declare what the ruler would do. This typically meant protecting the people against outside elements (but of course included conscripting his own people in order to defend or extend his boundaries). The covenant was heavily weighted in favor of the ruler. But astonishingly, the God of Israel was a forgiving God, a God who understood fickle human nature, and a God who declared in an unprecedented fashion, "Can a mother forget her nursing child, . . . ? / yet I will not forget you" (Isa 49:15). And perhaps even more surprising, the God of Israel frequently "repents" (or "relents" in some modern translations). God is willing to reconsider, to negotiate, to revoke threatened punishment, as is evident when Abraham asked if God will spare the people of Sodom if fifty honest people can be found. Not only does God accept Abraham's request, but five times more God accepts his further request for even greater mercy, until finally God says, "For the sake of ten I will not destroy it" (Gen 18:22-32). The God of Israel is clearly open to negotiation and heavily biased in favor of the chosen people.

So, God is a disturbing God who constantly communicates with the people, reminds them of their infidelity, calls them to repentance, and promises to accompany them forever. And yet God is not a God who coerces: God threatens *in order to call* people back to the covenant; but God does not force people. There is always the possibility that people might defect and abandon the covenant. God wants willing people, not people terrified into cowering obedience.

The God who disturbs but who does not coerce is not finished with God's people but invites them into a life-giving covenant: "You will be my people and I will be your God." Furthermore, God chooses to involve people in God's universal plan, calling the faithful to become, in effect, a Godly disturbance in the world. And this initiative is played out in the life and ministry of Jesus who calls and commissions disciples to become a Godly disturbance for the sake of the world. This is our call, today, in our particular circumstances: to be a Godly disturbance in the world—but definitely not an ungodly disturbance; there are far too many of those already.

(3) Sending or "Co-Missioning"

The final stage, at which a potential disciple is confirmed as an actual disciple, is when he or she follows Jesus on "the Way" or is sent, like the healed Gerasene demoniac (Mark 5:20) to the cities of the Decapolis or like the Samaritan woman (John 4:39) to evangelize her own people. The very purpose of the call/encounter and the disturbance/displacement is to move to this third stage. The rich man (Mark 10:17-22) was unable to negotiate the disturbance and "went away grieving," unable to follow Jesus at that time. Every would-be disciple must strive to be a missionary disciple, someone following the Way in the contemporary world. We are not in Palestine and not heading for Jerusalem, but by God's grace we are continuing the mission of Jesus, crossing boundaries not far from wherever we happen to be at any given moment, but in the name and by the "co-missioning" of Jesus.

Recontextualization or Application

If our reflections on New Testament accounts of the meeting of Jesus and a variety of individuals are not to become a purely academic or antiquarian exercise, we have to make some connections to our own lives. We are not the rich man or Bartimaeus of Mark 10, and we are not asked to imitate them slavishly. Our context and cultural circumstances are quite different from theirs. Discipleship entails responding to God's call in the particular circumstances of our own lives. There is no generic discipleship, because each person is specific and different. Therefore, making connections between the ancient text and our contemporary lives requires a little imagination on our part. We need to take some basic lessons and insights from these encounters and then formulate some questions that can challenge us to a more authentic following of Jesus as disciples of today. The process of recontextualizing—applying lessons from the New Testament to our personal lives—is in essence a process of faith formation, a way of deepening our faith through introspection and practice.

We already considered the importance of ears, and of listening, hearing, reflecting, and acting. Recontextualizing, or application, is a way to track what we have heard in the narratives and gauge whether and how the lessons of those narratives impinge on our own daily lives. Anyone who reads and ponders any of the New Testament stories of encounter or call, such as those in part 2 (though there are many more) should be able to generate a number of questions that would be pertinent to their own lives. From chapter 5 onwards, at the conclusion of the various stories explored, I list a number of questions that seem particularly relevant to me. They are only suggestions, and anyone with imagination can generate more. The important thing is that we do not simply read the stories—much less, superficially scan them because they are already familiar—and then move on to something completely different. Faith formation requires that we spend time with these stories in order to understand the nature of discipleship and attempt to cooperate with the initiative of Jesus Christ who calls each of us.

PART II

GOSPEL, DISCIPLESHIP, AND CONTEMPORARY LIVING

5

A Poor Rich Man
(Mark 10:17-22)

[17]As [Jesus] was setting out on a journey, a man ran up and knelt before him, and asked him, "Good Teacher, what must I do to inherit eternal life?" [18]Jesus said to him, "Why do you call me good? No one is good but God alone. [19]You know the commandments: 'You shall not murder; You shall not commit adultery; You shall not steal; You shall not bear false witness; You shall not defraud; Honor your father and mother.'" [20]He said to him, "Teacher, I have kept all these since my youth." [21]Jesus, looking at him, loved him and said, "You lack one thing; go, sell what you own, and give the money to the poor, and you will have treasure in heaven; then come, follow me." [22]When he heard this, he was shocked and went away grieving, for he had many possessions.

On the Way Again

It is a new day, and Jesus, always on "the Way" and having left Galilee, is working his way south—perhaps avoiding Samaria—and heading once again in the direction of Jerusalem. Accompanied by the Twelve—though at this point the text simply mentions an unspecified group of "disciples"—he sets off, but out of nowhere a man runs up to Jesus (clearly not going in the same direction as him) and throws himself at his feet. He does not "kneel," so much as (metaphorically) "bend the knee," which probably entails a preemptive lunge for Jesus' own knees or ankles. A person in immediate need of effective action from a patron or benefactor might grab such a person in this way, and plead his case. After the resurrection, Jesus met his disciples who "took hold of his feet" (Matt 28:8), which is essentially the same thing. Some commentators say it is a sign of discipleship, but in the case of the rich man, it is certainly pre-discipleship. Nevertheless, we have here a conventional gesture, understood by both parties: Jesus is now a captive audience and the man is the focus of attention.

The anonymous man wastes no time: "Good Teacher, what must I do to inherit eternal life?" he asks. His phrasing indicates that he believes eternal life is something apportioned by lot or divinely as-signed, and he wants some indication that he is a likely beneficiary. To address Jesus as "good Teacher" is a promising opener. "Teacher" may suggest that he sees himself as the other part of the dyad: a "learner" or (potential) disciple; and "good" is better than the con-ventional "sir." But it soon becomes clear that this man's problem or limitation is the fact that he asks, "What must *I* do?" as if eternal life is something he can achieve if he meets the qualifications and does so on his own initiative. But as we know, the *initiative* in dis-cipleship belongs to Jesus, and what he is looking for in potential disciples is an appropriate *response*. A problem for many people, perhaps even more today than in Jesus' time (and in the richer countries of the so-called First World), is that people are driven by personal initiative and ambition, and live in a world in which they believe they can achieve almost anything if they fully commit to it. But this is not the way of discipleship, and will not result in a person discovering the Way of Jesus. We may note at this juncture that although Jesus has not called the man explicitly, this is nevertheless an authentic encounter with Jesus, and thus the first stage on the way to discipleship.

Furthermore, it is the man who has opened the exchange, asking a very specific question: "What must I do?" He is looking for a recipe, an unequivocal answer to his burning question and a clear statement of precisely what is required of him: he is asking a "reli-gious" question. But Jesus never answers religious questions.

Second Temple Judaism—between 515 BCE and 70 CE—saw increased codification of laws and moral teachings, to the point where such legalism threatened to create a stratified society comprising (and opposing or polarizing) the good and the bad, the holy and the sinful, the respectable and the unrespectable. The effect of such "religion" and the "religious" questions it generated was to undermine people's freedom and overemphasize rule-keeping, obedience, and performance at the expense of a degree of spontaneity in worship and creativity in action. There were literally hundreds of religious questions, each with its own very specific answer, with the result that every loophole seemed to be covered, nothing was left to chance, and ambiguity was effectively erased. The law had, in consequence, become oppressive and burdensome to many, and great numbers of people—because of personal circumstances—were not even able to fulfill the religious requirements despite their good intentions. Into this environment, Jesus brought a decidedly different emphasis, refreshing and liberating for these many people, but iconoclastic and even sacrilegious in the view of some devout and punctilious observers of the law. His emphasis was not on the certainty and clarity and lack of ambiguity represented by formalized "religion" and its myriad rules, but on the possibilities, opportunities, and, frankly, the uncertainty or lack of clarity to be encountered in daily living. His alternative or complementary perspective (for he was a pious and respectful Jew himself) was that enlightened by "revelation."[1]

Where "religious" questions have—or where the enquirer seeks—specific, concrete answers (often referred to as the "W" questions: who, what, where, when—and how?), Jesus seeks to impart a glimpse of God's revelation—that is, of endless possibilities or opportunities for Godly action. Often universal in scope, such responses can be a real revelation to the questioner. Some examples might help. "Teacher, . . . *what* must I do to inherit eternal life?" (Luke 10:25, italics added) is a "religious" question seeking a definite and unambiguous answer. At first sight, Jesus does appear to answer it with, "You shall love the Lord your God"—until he amplifies his answer by adding "with all your heart, and with all your soul, and with all your strength, and with all your mind." It is clear that there is simply no end to the scope of this commandment. But even then, Jesus is not finished, for he adds a part B: "and your neighbor as yourself" (v. 27b). Not surprisingly, given the context and the mood, the inquirer—in this case a lawyer—then asks yet another "religious" question: "And *who* is my neighbor?" (italics added). But again Jesus will not give a clear and bounded answer. Instead he says, as is his wont, that he will tell a story—in this case, the parable of the Good Samaritan—after which he leaves the legal expert with the astonishing "revelation" that there is literally no end, no limit, to the commandment or to the definition of neighbor.

Some Pharisees came to Jesus with a trick question about paying taxes to Caesar. They knew the law, the legal requirements, but asked Jesus a specifically religious question: *What* do you think about the application of the law (see Matt 22:17)? We know the sequel: Jesus asks to see a coin, identifies the image of the emperor, and says, "Give therefore to the emperor the things that are the emperor's, and to God the things that are God's" (Matt 22:21). This is indeed a real revelation for the legalists and strictly "religious" Pharisees. Anyone who looks carefully for questions thrown at Jesus that begin with one of the "W" words can see just how he finesses the "religious" question and offers a "revelation" response instead. There are many such examples, but a final one here is a question posed by Peter: "*How often* must I forgive?" (italics added). But before Jesus can reply, Peter tries to answer his own "religious" question with a "revelation" answer: "As many as seven times?" he asks, evidently expecting praise from Jesus. But this is still not enough for Jesus, who says, "Not seven times, but, I tell you, seventy-seven times" (Matt 18:21-22)—a revelation indeed!

Returning now to the rich man's religious question, Jesus palpably avoids giving a religious answer, asking a question of his own instead: "Why do you call me good? No one is good but God alone. You know the commandments" (Mark 10:18-19). But although this "good" man does indeed know the commandments, Jesus identifies them himself, by itemizing them selectively: he lists most, but not all, of the Ten Commandments. Why is this? The man has identified Jesus both as teacher and as good—not exactly a declaration of faith, but certainly along the right lines. Now Jesus seeks the further assurance that the man is not simply using conventional language in calling him "good": Does he have real faith, or at least a desire to know more about the God who is good, and about God's ways? Significantly, Jesus identifies all the "horizontal" commandments and omits all the "vertical" commandments. The former are those commandments that specifically identify a duty toward other people, while the latter refer directly to one's duties to God.

At this point it appears that Jesus is about to endorse the rich man's religious observance of the "horizontal" commandments, as a prelude to returning to a deeper discussion about the man's relationship to the One he had called "good" and Jesus had named as God. But the rich man forestalls him: "Teacher, I have kept all these since my youth," he says (Mark 10:20). Significantly, perhaps, the word "good" has now disappeared from his address, and the man's stance seems somewhat more restive and even a little defensive. More significantly, it will be the last word he utters: he has not come to articulate his faith by stages but moved from a promising identification of Jesus as a "good teacher" to a simple "teacher"—and then silence; this is his last word.

But Jesus' response is beautiful and touching, without a hint of reproach or criticism, not a trace of "woe to you who are rich" (Luke 6:24). Instead, "Jesus, looking at him, loved him"—a sentence of wonderful and lyrical simplicity and encouragement. Jesus clearly does not want this conversation to end, and he wants to respond to the man's genuine religious question—but with a "revelation" response. So once again he encourages the man, saying, "You lack one thing." What a deeply affirming statement! Far from indicating that the man has a long way to go (or "a lot to learn," like the little children), Jesus is saying that he is already not far off target. But what

Jesus says next is truly a revelation and a great shock: the "one thing" is not one simple, clear, unambiguous religious rule, such as the man is seeking, but it is truly a revelation. It consists of five different components, each one a commandment of radical significance: "Go, . . . sell, . . . give, . . . come, . . . follow me" (Mark 10:21).

Here is the second stage of discipleship: the disturbance or displacement; and clearly the man is stunned. The NRSV text says, "When he heard this, he was shocked." Other translations have "amazed, astonished, perplexed, grieved, sad, sorrowful, gloomy" or other synonyms—and we will note later that one or other of these words describes the almost standard response of the disciples—the Twelve—to the revelation of Jesus. These five imperatives constitute a life's commitment for a man who wanted to retain his own initiative. It is only now that he realizes what Jesus is doing—inviting him to discover and to deepen his relationship to God, and experience a radical life change. In fact the text says very pointedly, "When he *heard* this" (Mark 10:22). Until this point he had not heard because he had not been listening. He had been talking, asking, justifying, defending, but not listening. And those who do not listen will not hear, or internalize, or reflect, or change their course of action. Perhaps he wanted to know a little more *about* or from Jesus; but he was not ready or willing actually to come to *know* Jesus, which is what Jesus was offering him.

The final phrase is very telling: "he was shocked and went away grieving, for he had many possessions." He went *away*, says Mark: he came his way, and went his way, but did not come to or follow the Way of Jesus. He could not negotiate the disturbance or displacement that discipleship entailed and, consequently, was not ready at this juncture to be sent or commissioned by Jesus. Paradoxically, the precise reason for his grief was that "he had many possessions." Typically, people think that possessions bring happiness and consequently that lack of possessions brings grief. But here is a man in exactly the opposite situation: a man of possessions who is *thereby* grieving. There is a very precise English word to describe his situation: he is a miser, a person whose unhappiness is directly related to his possessions; he has many things but no human relationships, and that situation is dehumanizing and distressing.

This is a person who is not willing to become a "learner," a disciple. He wants a clear-cut, unambiguous answer to his own "religious" question, but he does not listen to and internalize what Jesus offers him. He does not have sufficient faith in Jesus, or openness to the "revelation" Jesus offers, a revelation of possibilities and new ways of living. Nor is he willing to cross boundaries (one of the characteristics of the ministry of Jesus and of any true disciple). So this very familiar "rich young man"—who is, in point of fact, no longer young, having spoken about his youth in the past tense (Mark 10:20)—is likewise not truly a rich man but sadly a "poor rich man" who goes on his way, alone, just as he arrived.

Recontextualization or Application[2]

1. Like the rich man, I too am a good [Christian, religious, single person, spouse]—aren't I?

2. Like the rich man, I too have kept the commandments—haven't I?

3. What is one thing that I would be prepared to admit I lack?

4. Will I ever surrender my initiative?

5. Can I accept a disturbance or displacement as part of my call to discipleship?

6. Do I really want to come to *know* Jesus (as an *apprentice* rather than only through academic knowledge)?

6

A Profile of Discipleship
(Mark 10:23-45)

Overview

In this chapter we will follow Jesus and the Twelve after they leave the disconsolate and "shocked" rich man. They are now back on the road—on "the Way"—with Jesus, heading for Jericho. This part of chapter 10 of Mark's gospel forms a very useful bridge between the story of the rich man and the story of Bartimaeus. It also affords Jesus quite a teaching moment with his inner group of disciples. We will explore this in five small sections of teachings or lessons by Jesus.

First Lesson:
The Human Impossibility of Discipleship (vv. 23-27)

> [23]Then Jesus looked around and said to his disciples, "How hard it will be for those who have wealth to enter the kingdom of God!" [24]And the disciples were perplexed at these words. But Jesus said to them again, "Children, how hard it is to enter the kingdom of God! [25]It is easier for a camel to go through the eye of a needle than for someone who is rich to enter the kingdom of God." [26]They were greatly astounded and said to one another, "Then who can be saved?" [27]Jesus looked at them and said, "For mortals it is impossible, but not for God; for God all things are possible."

Immediately after the rich man has gone his own way, Jesus addresses his disciples (in this case, the Twelve). What he says constitutes a profile of discipleship that is profoundly helpful for us, and the disciples' response shows us emphatically how far away they are from having the mind of Jesus. This of course is also of great help to us, as we struggle with concerns not so different from theirs. Mark's willingness to show the very human failures of the Twelve can be a great encouragement to the rest of us as we struggle to find and to remain faithful to the Way.

Jesus preempts his disciples' concerns by declaring that to "enter the kingdom of God" is far from easy. One of the impediments will be "wealth", as shown by the rich man's reaction to Jesus' invitation. But the disciples are by no means rich in the conventional sense, so why this insistence by Jesus? The answer will become clearer in due course, but evidently the human *attachment* to material goods is the problem here, certainly as far as the rich man was concerned. It was evidently the major impediment to his following Jesus, one that he would not and could not remove or resolve. The one thing between this man and his becoming a disciple was his vise-like addiction to his wealth. Unless and until whatever comes between Jesus and a potential disciple can be removed or overcome, true discipleship is not possible.

The phrase "the kingdom of God" needs very careful probing, which would take us too far afield. But it is a critically important image or notion for Jesus and for the Jewish people of his time. He takes these words—familiar since early Judaism—and gives them an urgent contemporary meaning relative to his own ministry. Briefly, "the focus is irreducibly future" but its "implications are pressingly present"; and the ministry of Jesus has "a characteristic attitude of expectancy in respect of the future and, consequently, of responsibility within the present."[1] The remarks of Jesus indicate that a present attitude is as significant as a pious future expectation: attachment *now* is an impediment to the in-breaking of "the kingdom" both in its future completion and in its present stirrings or intimations.

The disciples were "perplexed" by these words of Jesus, evidently because of their application to the rich man but perhaps also for the implications for their own lives, especially if they imagined that being associated with Jesus would bring fame and fortune. But Jesus insisted for a second time, now addressing them as "children," for they clearly still had an awful lot to learn. He is not finished, however: he will repeat the statement a third time, using an image of a camel and a needle that has "perplexed" not only his hearers but people of every subsequent generation. But Jesus likes to play with words and images that call people to think differently. True to form, when the disciples hear this they are even more astounded and astonished. They do not understand but at least their complacency about discipleship is disturbed, and their assumptions about their own privileged status are being shaken. They even start asking each other, Who can pass the discipleship test? But Jesus overhears them and gives them yet another shock: it is frankly impossible without the help of God. Jesus fixes them with an intense look, and declares again, "For mortals it is impossible." And yet this latest shock wave lasts only a moment; they will immediately try to claim special status.

Second Lesson: Special Treatment for Some? (vv. 28-31)

> [28]Peter began to say to him, "Look, we have left everything and followed you." [29]Jesus said, "Truly I tell you, there is no one who has left house or brothers or sisters or mother or father or children or fields, for my sake and for the sake of the good news, [30]who will not receive a hundredfold now in this age—houses, brothers and sisters, mothers and children, and fields, with persecutions—and in the age to come eternal life. [31]But many who are first will be last, and the last will be first."

Peter is not perhaps as much the self-appointed spokesperson as he is the most brash and unthinking among the group, but he claims to speak for them all: "Look!" (or "See here!"), he says to Jesus. And then very dramatically declares that "we have left *every-*

thing." Everything? Given their backgrounds, what exactly is this "everything"—leaky boats and sweaty bodies, stinking fish and rotting nets, and tedious and predictable lives? They could hardly wait to drop their nets and leave their boats, caught up in the spirit of adventure and the charismatic personality of Jesus. And now Peter is grandstanding and claiming heroic virtue for himself and the rest. But Jesus does not remonstrate; he encourages them with the promise of massive compensation. But he also interjects—almost smuggles in—two warnings or promises that shock them even more. In what is sometimes referred to as "the famous Mark 10:30," Jesus promises persecutions along with rewards. And he is specific: this is not merely a possibility; there *will* be persecutions (notwithstanding the Jerusalem Bible "and not without persecutions" which softens it somewhat). The second caveat or warning is about a coming reversal of fortunes: many of those who consider themselves, or who are considered by others, to be "first" will be "last," while the insignificant nobodies will be elevated. He does not go into any detail, but his words have a devastating effect on the disciples.

Third Lesson: Painful Details (vv. 32-34)

> [32]They were on the road, going up to Jerusalem, and Jesus was walking ahead of them; they were amazed, and those who followed were afraid. He took the Twelve aside again and began to tell them what was to happen to him, [33]saying, "See, we are going up to Jerusalem, and the Son of Man will be handed over to the chief priests and the scribes, and they will condemn him to death; then they will hand him over to the Gentiles; [34]they will mock him, and spit upon him, and flog him, and kill him; and after three days he will rise again."

This is now the third installment of Jesus' instructions; and for Peter and those who are already thinking of themselves as the "first," it is by far the biggest shock so far. Mark, the evangelist, reminds us one more time that they are "on the road" or on the Way to Jerusalem, the climax of Jesus' ministry. Jesus is walking ahead, as he usually does, inviting others to follow him. But on this occasion, the "others" are experiencing the impact of the disturbance or displacement that discipleship entails, and they are totally unprepared for it. The Twelve are once again amazed (as in v. 24), but Jesus is attracting something of a crowd, and Mark now mentions "those who followed": they, too, are afraid, on the edge of panic after what Jesus has just said. Evidently at least some of them will not continue to be followers of Jesus. But Jesus addresses himself only to the Twelve now, as he tells them in vivid and explicit terms (v. 33) what will happen when they reach Jerusalem. They find it quite unthinkable, but it provides food for deep thought or at least silence and introspection. This is the most momentous statement imaginable, and one would think the disciples would protest vehemently—as Peter would, shouting "God forbid it, Lord!" when Jesus delivered the same news according to Matthew's account (Matt 16:22)—or at least be reduced to silence. But they do neither, and their response is quite outrageous in the circumstances.

Fourth Lesson: Misplaced Ambition (vv. 35-40)

> [35]James and John, the sons of Zebedee, came forward to him and said to him, "Teacher, we want you to do for us whatever we ask of you." [36]And he said to them, "What is it you want me to do for you?" [37]And they said to him, "Grant us to sit, one at your right hand and one at your left, in your glory." [38]But Jesus said to them, "You do not know what you are asking. Are you able to drink the cup that I drink, or be baptized with the baptism that I am baptized with?" [39]They replied, "We are able." Then Jesus said to them, "The cup that I drink you will drink; and with the baptism with which I am baptized, you will be baptized; [40]but to sit at my right hand or at my left is not mine to grant, but it is for those for whom it has been prepared."

In the very next verse, after Jesus has delivered the most dire and shocking news, James and John proceed to ask a favor that is not only grossly inappropriate but indicates that they have simply not been listening at this critical time. The best that can be said is that they at least address Jesus as "Teacher," but they are far from being what every teacher looks for: willing learners or disciples. They do have a question for him, but a totally inappropriate one: they want to jump ahead to the glory days.

What follows is a very telling example of the editorial hand of the various evangelists. Mark, who gives us this text, tends, as we noted, to show the disciples with their very human failings and rarely spares their blushes, while Matthew often makes excuses or omits certain details. In Matthew's account of this very same incident, it is the mother who is blamed for pushing her sons forward at this point! Matthew has just written that Jesus took the Twelve "by themselves" (Matt 20:17), yet the mother now suddenly appears out of nowhere (20:20-22).

In Mark's account, though, the egregious James and John do not even have the wit to blush at their totally inappropriate expectations. Yet once again Jesus shows remarkable forbearance, asking what they want him to do. He has not even mentioned glory (though he did make the gnomic, incomprehensible statement about rising again), but they want to bypass the extreme suffering and death he has just described, and they can visualize only his triumph. Not only have they failed to listen or hear, but now they appear to have heard what Jesus simply did not say. Their question demonstrates their arrogant immaturity and selective deafness (in striking contrast to Bartimaeus, to whom Jesus addresses exactly the same question, see chap. 7). Bartimaeus asked for nothing more than restoration to human dignity; James and John seek privilege and preferential treatment.

Jesus simply says that they do not know what they are asking. Or, as we might say, "they do not know what they're talking about." Certainly, they have no idea about the implications of the question. Jesus tries to identify some: drinking the cup that he is drinking, or being baptized with the baptism with which he is baptized. Yet without hesitation, and with even less thought, they respond in naive harmony, "We are able!" The only thing Jesus will say at this point is something to the effect of "you have no idea—you simply cannot imagine—what you will end up doing!" And he concludes the conversation by avoiding making any further predictions or promises.

Fifth Lesson: The First Will Be Last (vv. 41-45)

> [41]When the ten heard this, they began to be angry with James and John. [42]So Jesus called them and said to them, "You know that among the Gentiles those whom they recognize as their rulers lord it over them, and their great ones are tyrants over them. [43]But it is not so among you; but whoever wishes to become great among you must be your servant, [44]and whoever wishes to be first among you must be slave of all. [45]For the Son of Man came not to be served but to serve, and to give his life a ransom for many."

The other ten apostles, who often fail to listen or to hear, are now "all ears"; moreover they are angry with James and John ("indignant" is closer to the Greek verb). Found approximately seven times in the New Testament, this response is twice identified as that of Jesus himself—when he drives the money changers from the temple (John 2:13-17), and when he criticizes his disciples for discriminating against the "little children" who are so dear to him (Mark 10:13). As such, it is righteous or Godly indignation. But the other five occasions describe the reaction either of the synagogue leaders or the Twelve themselves, and in each of these cases their indignation is self-righteous and decidedly ungodly (see chaps. 8, 9).

On this occasion, the anger or indignation of the ten apostles is far from the righteous indignation characteristic of Jesus; this is self-righteousness, due to the fact that the sons of Zebedee stole their thunder. They would dearly have liked the "glory places" at Jesus' right and left. But on this occasion Jesus' response is directed at the two brothers, so the ten are saved this particular embarrassment.

In this fifth and final lesson, Jesus marks the striking contrast that should separate true disciples from "Gentiles." The latter—sometimes envied by Jews—are ruled by tyrants. But disciples of Jesus, like Jesus himself, must discover the "reversals" Jesus identifies: the "first" must become the "last," masters must become servants. The verb in verse

43 is in the future tense: "It *will not be* so among you"; evidently, they still have a lot to learn and a long way to go. Jesus now makes a contrast between a *doulos*, a slave or servant who has absolutely no choice but to act in a servile manner, and a *diakonos*, a term that denotes not status as such, but function. In other words, a *diakonos* chooses or undertakes acts of service, but is not forced to do so. Jesus says he will not call his disciples *doulos/douloi* but friends (*philoi*). He has already called them to be *diakonoi* (Mark 9:36) when they had recently been arguing about which of them was the greatest, saying, "Whoever wants to be first must be the last of all and *diakonos* of all." Evidently that advice had gone in one ear and out the other. Now he uses the same word and virtually the same phrase. Employing a little hyperbole, he uses the word *doulos* in verse 45. But when he says, in the following verse, that he himself came not to be served but to serve, he again uses the verbal form of *diakonos*, indicating that his service—like that he expects of his disciples—is freely chosen and not imposed. He closes this final teaching moment by stating that his own service will be at the cost of his own life.

Recontextualization or Application

1. If discipleship is "impossible" for mortals, left to their own initiative and determination, what is being asked of me at this moment (vv. 23-27)?

2. What is the "everything" that I like to claim I have left in order to follow Jesus (vv. 28-31)?

3. Am I still capable of being "amazed" or "afraid" of the cost of discipleship (vv. 32-34)?

4. What kind of recognition would I *not* dare to ask of Jesus at this point in my life (vv. 35-40)?

5. When have I acted like a *doulos*, from coercion or obligation alone? When do I act like a *diakonos*, by choosing to serve others (vv. 41-45)?

7

A Rich Poor Man
(Mark 10:46-52)

[46]They came to Jericho. As [Jesus] and his disciples and a large crowd were leaving Jericho, Bartimaeus son of Timaeus a blind beggar, was sitting by the roadside. [47]When he heard that it was Jesus of Nazareth, he began to shout out and say, "Jesus, Son of David, have mercy on me!" [48]Many sternly ordered him to be quiet, but he cried out even more loudly, "Son of David, have mercy on me!" [49]Jesus stood still and said, "Call him here." And they called the blind man, saying to him, "Take heart; get up, he is calling you." [50]So throwing off his cloak, he sprang up and came to Jesus. [51]Then Jesus said to him, "What do you want me to do for you?" The blind man said to him, "My teacher, let me see again." [52]Jesus said to him, "Go; your faith has made you well." Immediately he regained his sight and followed him on the way.

The five-component teaching module that Jesus has just imparted to the Twelve (Mark 10:23-45) forms a bridge between two stories that are almost mirror images of each other (see chap. 5). The anonymous rich man (who did not listen or hear and went away sad) is now contrasted with the named poor man who listened intently and went away happy. Mark has created a highly effective and subtle piece of writing in which, not only these two characters are contrasted, but their stories are placed like two bookends between which Jesus' instructions on discipleship itself are set. Not only does this serve to contrast the rich man and Bartimaeus, it is also illustrates exactly at what stage of faith and discipleship the Twelve have reached: they have been called and have encountered Jesus, but they are not negotiating the displacement and disturbance very well, and so at this stage they are far from being sent or co-missioned by Jesus. The Teacher was instructing the learners—his disciples—on the road, on "the Way" to Jerusalem. Now they arrive at Jericho, but Mark's narrative continues without giving any attention to that city; the group appears to be back on the road, on the Way to Jerusalem, immediately. But the text now speaks of "a large crowd," so evidently it includes more people than had already gathered on the road, previously identified simply as "those who followed" (v. 32). Scholars suggest that at this point there might have been perhaps fifty people in all. Jesus is presumably in the middle, surrounded by the Twelve and some thirty or forty others. They were "on the road" again, on the Way to a destiny; and a group of this size—probably no more than fifty—filled the roadway.

The blind beggar was, notes Mark, "sitting by the roadway." He was not, therefore, on the road, or the Way of discipleship, but at this point parallel to it. And as we know, parallel lines cannot converge—unless at least one of them moves. This is effectively what will happen as Jesus and Bartimaeus come face to face at the edge of the road, whereupon Bartimaeus "sprang up and came to Jesus"; and in their meeting Bartimaeus's life is changed forever.

The rich man had high status but no clear identity; he was not named. By contrast, the beggar has very low status—in fact, no social standing at all: he is "socially dead." But he is named. And the name he is given is not a personal name but a patronymic—the name of his father. We do not know his first name; only that he is "son of Timeus." But this is considerably more than we know about the rich man. It may indicate that although he seems to be a "nobody" now, it was not always so; once he could see, and once he had a family—a father called Timeus, and therefore a mother, and most probably siblings. As someone who is now socially dead, as good as dead, or "dead man walking," he is a pariah, avoided by respectable people and conventionally regarded as contaminated and a source of contamination. But, curiously and without further explanation, Mark gives us his father's name, Timeus, which is a name to be found nowhere else in the entire New Testament or in the intertestamental literature. And what appears to be the root of the word *timē* happens to be the Greek word for "honor." And if we add a Latinate ending, "us/a," we get Timē-us: an honorable man. This is only a guess, but Mark pays great attention to apparently insignificant details, and perhaps he is subtly naming the beggar as "bar-timeus"—the son of an honorable man—to indicate that he is not totally anonymous and bereft. Later in this story and in others, this hypothesis becomes even more of a possibility (see chap. 8).

Bartimaeus's very first action is to listen, to hear, and to respond: precisely the qualities Jesus is looking for. But that was literally the very last thing the anonymous rich man did ("When he heard this, he was shocked and went away grieving," v. 22), and it makes all the difference in the world to a blind man. Evidently he could not see Jesus—and would not have been able to see him even if there had not been a crowd of people *in the way* (the play on words here is significant). But he can listen—and if he actually hears the voice of Jesus, he will know exactly where its source is, and will be able to orient himself accordingly. And what better way to attract the attention of someone in the crowd and to provoke that person to speak than to shout out his or her name? That is exactly what Bartimaeus does. He had heard from others (v. 47) that it was Jesus of Nazareth, and he began to shout at the top of his voice, "Jesus, Son of David, have mercy on me!" What a mouthful! What an indication of his fledgling faith! The rich man addressed Jesus respectfully but conventionally as "good Teacher" but Bartimaeus has a much stronger, triple form of address.

First, he shouts Jesus' own name. To know a person's name and to name a person are indications of intimacy and even power. God gave the man, *'adam*, authority to name all the animals and birds (Gen 2:19), and the Gospel of Matthew says that the angel gave

Joseph authority to name Jesus (Matt 1:21). Though men rather than women name other persons or things, Elizabeth, John the Baptist's mother—and not Zechariah his father—names her son John (Luke 1:60). And it is also—unusually and significantly—Mary whom Gabriel instructs to name Jesus (Luke 1:31). To name someone can be an honor, a privilege, a right, or an indication of a relationship: Bartimaeus is clearly looking for some kind of relationship, calling Jesus by name. But he then identifies Jesus as "Son of David," a messianic title. Of itself it may not indicate that Bartimaeus has as yet come to faith, since it was used in various ways, and often with political or military connotations. But it does indicate that to Bartimaeus Jesus was someone of whom he had already heard and someone he regarded as special. However, it is the next phrase, "Have mercy on me," that is the best indication of his faith. Mercy is a divine attribute (whereas pity is equally a human attribute), and Bartimaeus identifies Jesus as one who can show mercy and not simply pity. Cumulatively, then, this triple form address is considerably more faith-driven than was the rich man's.

The immediate reaction of "many" of the crowd—and from this, and other more explicit passages, we may infer that the Twelve are certainly prominent among them—"sternly ordered him to be quiet." They attempt to block Bartimaeus's access to Jesus: an example of the times the "institution" (here the Twelve) gets in the way of the "charism" (Jesus). It happens several times in the gospels and many times throughout the history of the church. But Bartimaeus is not going to let this opportunity—his best and perhaps his only one left—pass; and "he cried out even more loudly, 'Son of David, have mercy on me!'" He has dropped the name of Jesus but repeats the specific titles he has just used; this is yet more evidence of his conviction and his fierce and courageous faith.

Now, in contrast to what happened with the rich man, Jesus stops and calls to him via the crowd: "Call him here," he says. And the very people who interfered without any authority to do so now change their tune abruptly and attempt to win the favor of Jesus, saying to the blind man in a rather condescending manner, "Take heart; get up, he is calling you." Of course Bartimaeus exhibits far more courage than those who presume to encourage him! But here we have, very clearly, a call from Jesus—in contrast to the case of the rich man who was not called but ran up and encountered Jesus on his own initiative. The scene is now set for the second stage of discipleship: the disturbance or displacement. This, for Bartimaeus, is the moment of truth, and Jesus has explicitly called him. Some of the Twelve had also done so, and therefore the crowd will have opened up so that there is no longer any impediment, any blockage, to his access. Granted that Bartimaeus cannot see Jesus, nevertheless he has heard his voice so he knows exactly where Jesus is. Nothing will stop him now—except the awful possibility that he might trip over his cloak and fall on his face. All he has to do is quickly gather his cloak about him and close the gap between himself and Jesus. But what he actually does is, under the circumstances, unexpected, startling, and objectively quite shameful.

Bartimaeus is a blind beggar, and as such owns virtually nothing—and perhaps literally nothing—but his cloak. The book of Exodus suggests as much: "If you take your neighbor's cloak in pawn, you shall restore it before the sun goes down; for it may be your neighbor's only clothing to use as cover; in what else shall that person sleep?" (Exod 22:26-27; also Deut 24:12-13). A person who needs to retrieve a cloak in such circumstances must therefore own virtually nothing. So under his cloak, Bartimaeus is very likely naked or virtually so; to jettison one's cloak in public would be a shameful thing to do.

The "social currency" of the world on whose margins Bartimaeus lives is the attribute or virtue of honor. But as with credit and debt, so with honor and shame: the more honor one can accrue, the less shame one suffers, and vice versa. An increase in shame means a concomitant loss of honor. But as a blind beggar, Bartimaeus is a nobody with no social currency at all; therefore he has absolutely nothing to lose. He may indeed have been called, after his father, "son of an honorable man," but as far as his "honor account" is concerned, he is at this moment, bankrupt. Therefore what would be shameful for a man of honor[1] (to expose his nakedness in public) is of no consequence to Bartimaeus. The only thing on his mind is to get to Jesus. Therefore the cloak *must* go.

Mark is the storyteller here, of course, and Mark may have had particular reason to mention the detail about the cloak and Bartimaeus's assumed nakedness. In Mark's account of the passion and death of Jesus, he notes that a young man was following the soldiers when they apprehended Jesus (Mark 14:51-52). Curiously, this "young man" was wearing only a linen cloth, and as Jesus was seized, he ran off, leaving the cloth behind: "and he was naked." Commentators surmise that this young man was Mark himself, and his nakedness symbolizes his shame at abandoning Jesus to his captors.

To return to Bartimaeus—in pointed contrast to the naked man who was shamed—"throwing off his cloak, he sprang up and came to Jesus." These three verbs say so much: he *threw off* his cloak; he *sprang up*; and he *came* to Jesus. The verb for "to throw off" implies there is no chance of recovery: this is total commitment. The verb "to spring up" is used of a person; if it is used of a wellspring, it is a different verb with the same meaning—the verb, in fact, that Jesus uses when promising the woman at the well, "living water springing up to eternal life" (John 4:14). Finally, of course, he "came to Jesus" implies much more than physical movement: it is the convergence of two lives, and the connection of previously parallel lines.

The question Jesus poses tells us as much about Jesus as the answer does about Bartimaeus. A benefactor who *tells* the beneficiary what he or she intends to do (and expects gratitude) is taking a (perhaps commendable) *initiative* but remains in control of the situation. A compassionate person who *asks* someone what he or she needs is ceding control but showing a willingness to offer an appropriate *response* to the other's need. It is far easier to do things for others and to *tell* them what we will do (and expect them to be grateful) rather than to *ask* them, and thus risk their unpredictable response.

Jesus the teacher takes the initiative in calling and commissioning learners/disciples; but Jesus the servant is ready to respond appropriately to whomever he serves. So he asks Bartimaeus, "What do *you* want *me* to do for you?" And Bartimaeus rises magnificently to the occasion, not asking for anything shallow or flamboyant, but simply identifying what was at the core of every faithful Jew's hope: *restoration* of Israel's fortunes and of its people's dignity. This was exactly what Jesus had promised when he articulated his own "mission statement" in the synagogue at Jerusalem (see Luke 4:16-20 and, especially, Isa 61:1-4, which Jesus is reading from at the time). So Bartimaeus simply asks for the *restoration* of his humanity—his dignity—that has been stripped away because of his blindness, his poverty, and a theology that Jesus has come to identify as deeply flawed. "My teacher, let me see *again*," says the blind man. "My teacher," he says; not simply "teacher" or even "good teacher" like the rich man. The Greek text actually uses the exact word that Mary Magdalene used on the day of the resurrection—*Rabboni.* "My teacher" is a faith statement and an expression of discipleship.

The next and final thing Jesus says is "Go!" He does not say, "Fine! I will do a miracle," nor does he draw attention to himself. Because his primary interest is identifying or sowing seeds of faith in the people he encounters, he says, "Your *faith* has made you well." It is already in the past tense: Bartimaeus can already see. Jesus has not touched him but publicly acknowledged his healing. The way Mark—and both Matthew and Luke borrow this on occasion—suggests that there is no gap between faith and miracle, or between Jesus' act and its effect, is to insert the word "immediately." So the two sentences of the text can be run together as: "Jesus said to him, 'Go; your faith has made you well'; immediately he regained his sight." And the final phrase is the perfect, condensed phrase that illustrates discipleship: "and followed him on the way." The way of discipleship is the Way of Jesus, and it leads to Jerusalem.

Recontextualization or Application

1. Where would I situate myself at this moment—on the Way or by the wayside? Do I feel perhaps that I have lost my way, or that I am actually in the way?

2. What is blocking my access to Jesus? Who or what is getting "in the way"?

3. Am I aware of my "blind spots"? What am I doing to compensate?

4. What is the "cloak" that I cling to and am afraid to "throw off"? Why am I afraid?

5. What do I *really* want, from God, from others, and perhaps even from myself?

8

A Bent-Over Woman
(Luke 13:10-17)

[10]Now [Jesus] was teaching in one of the synagogues on the sabbath. [11]And just then there appeared a woman with a spirit that had crippled her for eighteen years. She was bent over and quite unable to stand up straight. [12]When Jesus saw her, he called her over and said, "Woman, you are set free from your ailment." [13]When he laid his hands on her, immediately she stood up straight and began praising God. [14]But the leader of the synagogue, indignant because Jesus had cured on the sabbath, kept saying to the crowd, "There are six days on which work ought to be done; come on those days and be cured, and not on the sabbath day." [15]But the Lord answered him and said, "You hypocrites! Does not each of you on the sabbath untie his ox or his donkey from the manger, and lead it away to give it water? [16]And ought not this woman, a daughter of Abraham who Satan bound for eighteen long years, be set free from this bondage on the sabbath day?" [17]When he said this, all his opponents were put to shame; and the entire crowd was rejoicing at all the wonderful things that he was doing.

In the New Testament accounts we find Jesus teaching in synagogues more than a dozen times: in Nazareth, Capernaum, and other unspecified locales. As someone who must have received an invitation from a synagogue official before he could take on a formal role, Jesus was becoming increasingly widely known, both directly and by repute. The location of the synagogue featured in this account is not specified. A synagogue, unlike the temple, was a place of assembly and not always even a building, but men and women were not strictly segregated, and God-fearing Gentiles were often present, too. It is, as usual, the Sabbath day.

Commentators note that English translations of verse 11 are not always precise. "And a woman was there" (NABRE, JB) does not do justice to the Greek text. "And behold, there was a woman" (KJB, NASB) rightly indicates that readers should pay attention ("Behold!"); but "there was a woman" or "a woman was there" can sound rather inconsequential, when Luke's emphasis is on her commitment, determination, and steadfast faith. The text actually reads, "And behold, a woman *was*." The verb, significantly, is in the imperfect tense or continuous past: she was not there by happenstance; she was there intentionally and was profoundly present. This commitment, of course, makes all the difference to Jesus and, in a moment, to her. It is an indication of her faith and steadfastness.

Luke—traditionally understood to have been a physician—adds important details. The diagnosis that makes her, like Bartimaeus, "socially dead" is her "spirit of weakness," ostensibly caused by a demon; its symptoms are that she is crippled and has been so for eighteen years.[1] But apart from being a true description of this woman's physical state, the detail that "she was quite unable to stand up straight" describes someone regarded as less than human, less than bipedal and upright. But it is to precisely such persons as this that Jesus has come, in order to bring them, like Bartimaeus, to *restoration* (or liberation: one of the integral components of the evangelizing ministry and mission of Jesus[2]). In a society where the life expectancy is considerably less than thirty-five years,[3] her condition has thoroughly compromised this woman's entire life, for even if she is in her thirties she is unlikely ever to have been married, produced any children, or given and received human touch or affection. This is truly a profile of social death, and very significant for our understanding and appreciation of the implications of these "eighteen years."

Furthermore, as anyone in a similar condition is aware—or as any of us, willing to bend over for a few minutes—one's field of vision extends in a radius of only about six feet; one is unable to look up at other people's faces, and everyone literally looks down on such a sad figure. And since Jesus is, of course, teaching or preaching in the synagogue in an official role, this woman, already bent over and most likely further marginalized by her gender, would not have taken a prominent place and would therefore not be immediately visible to the casual observer. She is truly marginalized.

This makes it even more remarkable that Jesus even saw her. But as soon as he did, he called her over. We might imagine the frisson of excitement and anticipation in the congregation: it is the Sabbath day, in the middle of a service, and everything has come to a halt as the woman is called by Jesus. And then, infinitely slowly, she shuffles toward him, while every eye is on her and Jesus. But the anticipation and expectation on the part of those who sympathized with Jesus would be more than matched by the rapidly accumulating discomfort of the synagogue officials that rapidly turned from shock and frustration to rage and "indignation" at the action of Jesus. But what happened next was utterly unforeseeable. With no further preamble and without laying a hand on her, Jesus declares for all to hear, "Woman, you are set free from your ailment."

To begin a sentence with, or to address someone as, "woman" sounds strange, if not offensive, to modern ears. Jesus does it at the outset of his public life at Cana, when he addresses his mother with a question, "Woman, what concern is that to you and to me?" (John 2:4). The vocative case translates as "O woman," a term of respectful address. Used here, it is a particularly striking indication of Jesus' sensitivity toward the broken woman before him. And immediately afterwards he declares unequivocally, "You are set free from your ailment"; and the implication is unmistakable.

No pious Jew would dare to use God's name directly, because the third commandment strictly forbade it (Exod 20:7; Deut 5:11). So Jesus simply could not have said, "God"—as in Yhwh, *Jehovah*, *Adonai*, or another name for God—"has healed you." The generic word for God (*theos*) was sometimes used, but the only other possibility and the standard convention for attributing some action specifically to God's intervention was to use a "divine passive," which neatly avoids naming the subject but leaves everyone in no doubt that the subject is God. "You are set free from your ailment" is such a divine passive. It is also couched in the past tense, signifying that it has already happened, as was the case for Bartimaeus: it is a *fait accompli*. And yet at this point Jesus himself has not touched the woman. But as soon as he makes this declaration he reaches out to her, and Luke borrows Mark's convention of using the word "immediately": "When he laid his hands on her, *immediately* she stood up straight and began praising God."

But there is a difficulty here. If the woman has already been declared healed by God, why would Jesus "lay his hands on her"? We are familiar with this action from other stories, and it is easy to imagine that Jesus always does this as a sign of his healing. But in this instance Jesus has *not* healed her, and has clearly identified his *Abba* as the healing agent. So what is happening? First, we should recall the setting: the synagogue, the Sabbath, and every eye riveted on what is happening. Some in the congregation are amazed and impressed, while others are in deep consternation. And Jesus is standing, in public, before a woman understood to be socially dead and therefore to be strictly avoided—a woman who has not felt human touch or affection for eighteen years—*and laying his hands on her.*[4]

Conventional ideas of Jesus extending both hands over this woman's head in a ritualized act of exorcism are quite inappropriate and fanciful here. Jesus is very tactile and affectionate, exactly what this woman needs at this point in her life. To declare her to be healed already but then to walk away from her would be heartless and completely unlike Jesus. Surely, then, he puts his arms *around* her, embracing, enfolding, hugging her. And in response (again prefaced by the word "immediately") "she stood up straight." The immediacy with which she becomes upright, restored to her humanity and standing straight, links the action of God, the action of Jesus, and her own reaction as taking place simultaneously.

Luke's next phrase is particularly interesting: "she began praising God." Why does he not tell us what she said or what she was thinking? Surely she is not silent at this moment? Of course her most natural response is to luxuriate in her newfound physical freedom. Semi-paralyzed for more than half a lifetime, she suddenly has the use of limbs—of her entire body—such that she had not known for years. So she must be dancing, spontaneously praising God (not only, as Mary, whose "soul magnifie[d] the Lord," Luke 1:46) with her entire self, body and soul. There is a telling incident in the Acts of the Apostles when Peter and John encounter a lame man. After he is healed "in the name of Jesus Christ," the man "jumped up and went into the temple with them, walking and leaping and praising God" (Acts 3:6-8). This immediately resonates with the story of the broken woman.

One of Daniel O'Leary's consistently soul-feeding and lyrical pieces contains these lines:

> "When grace enters" wrote W. H. Auden, "humans must dance." And when does grace enter? It enters when, for instance, I make the choice each morning to live freely today rather than exist like a victim, to run the way of beauty rather than stumble along the blind way. When I begin to believe that God is holding on to me, no matter what—I want to dance.
>
> A kairos time and time for dancing is when we begin, after many years, to live our unlived lives, so as to die without regret. We create a tiny dance floor when we hold off, even for a split second, these dark and deadly thoughts . . . We can dance in that space because in it we have regained our blessed balance, our divine energy. This space may last the length of a human breath, but it hides and reveals the heart of redemption.
>
> Something in all of us wants to dance when courage taps us on the shoulder, when the chains of fear and the baggage of false guilt fall from our shoulders. We want to dance when we feel a passion for the possible, when we hear the music of hope. . . . The time to dance is now.[5]

Into this joyful and liberating hubbub strides the leader of the synagogue, looking to put a stop to the celebration and "indignant because Jesus had healed on the Sabbath." Strictly speaking, Jesus did no such thing: he deferred explicitly to a divine act caused by his *Abba*. But this is a detail. The leader's pretext for his indignation (as we noted already—see the apostles' similar reaction in the previous chapter—an example of self-righteous rather than Godly indignation) is that it is happening on the Sabbath day, a day when no work should be done. Evidently, what had just happened was identified by the leader as work done by Jesus. Apart from observing that such a definition of "work" was religious legalism at its worst, and that Jesus had no truck with such sophistry, there are two other things that provoke Jesus to characterize the synagogue leaders as "hypocrites": first, the leader is appealing "to the crowd" rather than having the courage or integrity to direct his words at Jesus or the woman directly (and we all know how cowardly we, too, can be when we act in a similar way because we lack the courage to confront a person directly); and second, the excuse itself is paper thin and yet another example of the kind of narrow and constricting religious legalism that Jesus has come to put under the lens of God's expansive and liberating revelation.

They appeal to the crowd for support, urging that the woman come on an ordinary day and not on the Sabbath day. But this woman has been *there*, profoundly and continually present over many, many weekdays and Sabbaths. Yet no one appears even to have noticed her, much less to have reached out with compassion. The leader evidently operates with a set program, a routine with no flexibility. Jesus, of course, has no set program, only an open pastoral approach to anyone and everyone, and his flexibility is total. And he calls the leaders—all of them, guilty by association—"hypocrites," the most stinging criticism to be found on his lips anywhere in the New Testament, and more astringent than "brood of vipers" or even "whited sepulchers." Added to which, Jesus was adamant: "The sabbath was made for humankind, and not humankind for the sabbath" (Mark 2:27).

In the Greek language, the first meaning of the word we translate as hypocrite (Greek: *hupokritēs*) is a "stage actor," but it is also used metonymically, as in English and as it is here, to mean duplicitous or "two-faced." Greek theater did not use much in the way of scenery or props, but actors in togas or simple dress would wear masks to depict the characters they were portraying. Some people, of course, wear a metaphorical mask more permanently, hiding immorality behind a mask of respectability. Jesus is accusing the very religious officials of this kind of deception.

Having roundly criticized those who knew that they could "work" when caring for their livestock but would prohibit similar concern for a human being, Jesus uses another *divine passive* to underline a God's-eye perspective: "Ought not this woman . . . be set free?" "Don't you understand," he is saying in effect, "that God wants to care for people on the Sabbath and every other day?" He acknowledges that a spirit of weakness ("Satan") has held this woman in thrall, but not totally and not indefinitely: today is a new beginning for her, no longer a victim, as Daniel O'Leary puts it. But he endorses her even more explicitly by calling her a "daughter of Abraham." The synagogue officials consider themselves, and rightly so, as "sons of Abraham"; but perhaps they never thought of this woman, and if they did, they must have dismissed her as merely a woman (as many translations of verse 11 almost imply). Jesus is emphatic: she is a daughter of Abraham, every bit as significant as any of Abraham's sons! This remark, as well as the attitude of publicly shaming the officials, will cause them to focus on his downfall. But the final verse is even more telling: "When he said this, all his opponents were put to shame; and the entire crowd was rejoicing at all the wonderful things that he was doing."

Having been called hypocrites in public for their blatant double standards, the officials have been put to shame, and by their humiliation they have lost a significant amount of their social capital: their honor. They will not rest until they have made every effort to restore that honor. But Jesus has accomplished something else, without any grandstanding or drawing attention to himself. He has intentionally focused attention on the woman herself—and on the action of God.

So in what sense can we claim that she was, or was on the way to being, a disciple? She experiences a call from Jesus and responds immediately and without demur or question. She is certainly an example of someone honestly searching for God—seeking "the Way," not only implicitly but by her dogged determination. She was in fact still *there*, despite suffering for years. If not full-blown faith, this is certainly steadfast faithfulness, which is at least an honest search for and commitment to faith in God. And when she feels the healing in her body, her spontaneous reaction is to praise God. If we had as much integrity as she, we would certainly fit the description of a disciple.

A couple of final observations might be appropriate. First, Luke might have referred to "the congregation" or perhaps "the people" but the word he uses is *ochlos*: "the crowd" ("the whole crowd was rejoicing"). But not only does Jesus himself never criticize "the crowds"—as he does his own disciples—he consistently favors them: the nobodies, lower classes, ignorant, and decidedly *not* identified by members of the official class as "learners" or disciples. And second, it is precisely these nobodies who are to be found, in the synagogue, on the Sabbath, "rejoicing at all the wonderful things that [Jesus] was doing." The officials were blind, but the crowds could see plainly. This is an example of what is called the *sensus fidelium*, the instinct of ordinary decent people, for the things of God. Still—and this is re-grettable, since Luke is usually understood as the champion of women—Luke does not dignify her with the name "disciple."[6]

As for the "wonderful things" (v. 17), the word literally means things that are "notable" or "held in high repute." Evidently the people identified in Jesus a person who was not only good but exceptionally so. But since an almost identical reference occurs in the story we turn to next, we will consider it later.

Recontextualization or Application

1. "Behold! A woman was *there*," profoundly and faithfully present. Am I?

2. Where have I been for the past eighteen years—or for much of my life?

3. What causes me to be "bent over" and less than totally upright?

4. Do I praise God? How do I do this?

5. Do I even *want* to be restored, when it might be easier to do nothing, or simply complain?

A Memorable Evening
(Mark 14:3-9)

³While [Jesus] was at Bethany in the house of Simon the leper, as he sat at the table, a woman came with an alabaster jar of very costly ointment of nard, and she broke open the jar and poured the ointment on his head. ⁴But some were there who said to one another in anger, "Why was the ointment wasted in this way? ⁵For this ointment could have been sold for more than three hundred denarii, and the money given to the poor. And they scolded her. ⁶But Jesus said, "Let her alone; why do you trouble her? She has performed a good service for me. ⁷For you always have the poor with you, and you can show kindness to them whenever you wish; but you will not always have me. ⁸She has done what she could; she has anointed my body beforehand for its burial. ⁹Truly I tell you, wherever the good news if proclaimed in the whole world, what she has done will be told in memory of her.

This must be the most mangled and misunderstood story in the entire New Testament. There is a version in each of the four gospels, but the details and the lessons of each are by no means the same, and so, effectively, we have several different stories. Unfortunately, many of us have succeeded in unconsciously conflating the stories into a single narrative, but one that is not actually found in that form in any of the gospel accounts. Typically, the story comes to be reimagined as centering on a sinful woman called Mary Magdalene,

who washes the feet of Jesus, is forgiven, and becomes one of the
most faithful and committed of all the disciples of Jesus. So let us
state at the outset that the story we will now explore—found in the
Gospel of Mark, the first gospel to be written—is *not* about a sinful
woman. The (unnamed) woman is *not* Mary Magdalene, and she
does *not* wash the feet of Jesus! It was Pope Gregory the Great (d.
604) who misidentified the woman as Mary Magdalene (she is
anonymous in the synoptic accounts; in John she is named Mary *of
Bethany*). In popular imagination and much iconography, painting,
and literature, this confusion remains today, and it has obscured
and tarnished the legacy of Mary Magdalene, the first witness of the
resurrection and an outstanding disciple and apostle.[1]

Figure 4

SCRIPTURE	LOCATION	HOST(S)	RELATION-SHIP	THE WOMAN	THE ACTION
Mark 14:3-9	Bethany	Simon	A leper	Anonymous *holy* woman	*ON THE HEAD* "'poured' ointment of nard"
Matthew 26:6-13	Bethany	Simon	A leper	Anonymous *holy* woman	*ON THE HEAD* "'poured' ointment"
Luke 7:36-50	Unspecified	Simon	A Pharisee	Anonymous *sinful* woman	*ON THE FEET* "'bathed' with ointment"
John 12:1-8	Bethany	Martha and Mary	Friends	Mary (of Bethany)	*ON THE FEET* "'anointed' with nard"

The woman in Mark's account—to which Matthew's is almost
identical—is about an unnamed and unquestionably holy woman
whom Jesus commends in an unparalleled way, much to the dis-

comfort and even shame of the Twelve.[2] In Mark's account, this takes place "two days before the Passover" and immediately before Judas leaves to betray Jesus (Mark 14:10). It is therefore the passage that introduces the passion according to Mark on Passion Sunday. But before we look more closely at Mark's highly nuanced account, it might help to represent each of the stories in tabular form (fig. 4).

Mark's narrative opens with a very clear statement of what Jesus was doing, where, and with whom. Though he does not specify that the Twelve were the other people there (in v. 4, simply, "some were there"), this sounds very much like the Twelve, from what we know already about their behavior and their dilatoriness in learning the nature of discipleship. Jesus is described, pointedly, as "in the house of Simon the leper" (v. 3). Luke's account likewise identifies a man called Simon, but this one is "a Pharisee" (7:36, 40). For Jesus—and particularly these core disciples—to eat with a Pharisee would have been a perfectly respectable and even an upwardly mobile experience and quite a treat; but to eat with a leper would have been quite unheard of and scandalous, and the disciples would have been thoroughly unhappy. This was decidedly a gesture of downward mobility for anyone with ambition. The leper was socially dead, as were Bartimaeus (Mark 10:46-52) and the bent woman (Luke 13:10-17); to consort with such a person rendered one ritually unclean, and to sit down and eat with such a person was a blatant act of religious rule-breaking (see Lev 13; 14). Although Jesus said he had not come to change a "jot or a tittle" of the religious rules, he did, on occasion, flout them when they imposed unbearable burdens on others. He did this in order to illustrate the revelation, liberation, and restoration he was determined to propagate. Table-ministry was one of the most visible characteristics of the mission of Jesus, and arguably the main reason that ultimately got him killed.[3] We can imagine therefore that this would be at least a learning moment for the Twelve, though it turned out to be much more than they could possibly have imagined.

Having told readers or hearers about the kind of people Jesus frequently vistited (though an early tradition suggested that Simon was a *former* leper, already healed and ritually cleansed), Mark adds the critically important detail that Jesus was seated at the table (v. 3), a clear indicator of a person's social status or, in this case, a particular social role or chosen function. In Jesus' culture, the position of one's head relative to that of other people was socially significant, and we can identify three such positions. When my head is higher than yours, I am in the superior or superordinate position while you are my inferior or subordinate. Likewise, when my head is lower than yours, I am socially inferior or subordinate and you are superior. The third position would be where each of us is on the same level: we are equals, whether by social status or by convention. Sometimes and quite legitimately Jesus adopts the superior position, as when preaching in the synagogue or instructing his disciples (as their teacher). But he also frequently adopts the position of equality when eating with friends like Martha, Mary, and Lazarus, or with his own disciples—and here in the house of Simon the leper.

But on three very significant occasions Jesus deliberately adopts the position of a social inferior, and this fact is very pertinent. At the Last Supper he takes on the role of a servant, moving to wash the feet of the Twelve, during which activity his head is lower than theirs. Understandably, Peter is shocked at this gesture and in this context: sitting at table with Jesus is an activity Jesus and the inner group of disciples had become accustomed to, an arrangement of social equality. But footwashing was a servile gesture—the duty of a slave—and not that of a friend or equal. But we know the rest: Jesus insisted, Peter acquiesced, and Jesus told the disciples that they, in turn, *must* wash the feet of each "other" without limit.

The second occasion was no less striking. John's gospel is famous for its high Christology (Jesus seems to know everything all the time and is never outguessed). It is all the more striking, then, that John's gospel tells us very clearly that Jesus was passing through Samaria. "Jesus, tired out by his journey, was sitting by [Jacob's] well" (John 4:6) when a Samaritan woman came to draw water. No wonder she was also deeply shocked: from a sitting position, beneath her standing position, Jesus' head is clearly lower than hers, and he has no choice but to look up to her as she, perforce, looks down on him. He is ostensibly the social superior and she the inferior, he a Jew and she a renegade Samaritan, he a man and she a mere woman: *he* makes a request of *her*, thus inverting their social positions. Her shock quickly turns to apparent sarcasm as she observes momentarily that this stranger cannot even get himself a drink, much less give her "living water." But from these respective positions they move first to a dialogue of equals (she matches him step for step and point for point) and then to a real teacher/learner relationship: she becomes the first missionary disciple in the New Testament.

The third example is found here, in the story at the house of Simon the leper. Mark tells us that Jesus was sitting at the table when the woman came in. Evidently, then, her head was higher than his, and relative to her he is in the inferior position: How else would she have even been able to *reach* his head? In the stories recounted by Luke and John, the woman reaches for his feet, which is entirely possible for anyone willing and able to bend down and take the inferior position. Luke's anonymous sinful woman washes his feet with tears, and then anoints them with ointment (John says nard), but in both Luke's and John's accounts this is the act proper to a slave or servant. Not so in the case of this woman.

Far from acting spontaneously, she has gone to great pains in preparing for her shocking intervention. She is carrying "an alabaster jar" filled with "very costly ointment of nard" (v. 3). "Alabaster" is simply the Greek word for "without handles," but it also describes a particular kind of flask or container of unguents with special functions associated with massage and embalming. Ointment or perfume made from nard or spikenard had to be kept in a tightly sealed container, and to unseal the container was referred to as "breaking the [seal of the] jar." Nard itself was a precious and expensive aromatic herb used all over the ancient world. Its use in embalming seems to have been partly due to its very strong scent, strong enough to mask the decomposition of a corpse. Jesus clearly knew its use in that context. But Jesus is evidently not dead, and the woman poured the ointment on his head, an action very closely associated with a religious or ritual anointing, on which Jesus will also remark.

The ointment is identified as very costly, and the action of breaking the seal was an indication that this ointment was being used for a once-only occasion. Clearly the woman has prepared carefully, not only purchasing the ointment but determining the whereabouts of Jesus and then deciding to burst in, not only on a private dinner but on the residence of a leper, a pariah. This is not the behavior of a slave or a servant but a premeditated act of a highly motivated and determined woman of very considerable means. It is also, objectively, quite scandalous behavior. An unnamed and unknown woman appears to burst into a house and proceeds, without asking, to massage the head of Jesus with aromatic oil. It is certainly sensuous, and has what observers might easily conclude as highly intimate and sexually charged behavior. But Jesus does not flinch or resist; not only does he permit her action but immediately defends her from the outraged reaction of the rest of his company. His irritation is reserved for his disciples. Simon, the evening's host, says and does nothing, discretion being the better part, on this occasion.

Instantly, sadly, and rather predictably, some of the guests reacted. In Mark's words, they "said to one another in anger"[4] (v. 4) — virtually the same reaction as that of the synagogue officials in response to Jesus' treatment of the bent woman, and of the disciples' reaction to Bartimaeus (Mark 10:48). They murmur among themselves because they do not have the courage to face Jesus, and because they are volatile, immature, and judgmental. Their paper-thin reason for complaining is no better than that of the synagogue officials whom Jesus unequivocally called hypocrites. They are lucky not to be called the same when they say, "'Why was the ointment wasted in this way? For [it] could have been sold for more than three hundred denarii, and the money given to the poor.' And they scolded her" (vv. 4-5).

Three things are worth noting here: references to the disciples' outburst, to the cost of the ointment, and to "the poor." The disciples have no authority here, and yet their instinctive reaction is to murmur among themselves and then to presume to scold the woman (v. 5), using the same verb that expressed Jesus' own indignation at the disciples' callous treatment of the children. Clearly this is another example of their officious self-righteousness. Second, the reference to the ointment's cost of "three hundred denarii" indicates that they knew what a ceremonial alabaster jar and its contents were worth. The figure mentioned is equivalent today to an annual income for a wage earner: upwards of $25,000 or $30,000, and so substantial that the woman's gesture of conspicuous consumption or deliberate and dedicated "wastage" attests to her deep faith and commitment to Jesus—two of the marks of discipleship. Finally, the phrase, "the poor you have always with you" is often used as a lazy bromide, an excuse or justification for doing nothing. But this is not its real significance. When Jesus uses it (v. 7), he is not making it up, much less using it as an excuse for neglecting people. He is referring to the book of Deuteronomy, which explicitly states, "There will, however, be no one in need among you . . . if only you will obey the LORD your God by diligently observing [the law]" (Deut 15:4-5). These are Moses' words as he prepares the people to enter the Promised Land, where there will be enough for everyone—if each person lives according to God's law. Jesus is not accepting poverty as a social fact but reminding his disciples that it should not be the case among Godly people.

Immediately after the disciples' outburst comes the disturbance or displacement we identified earlier: the moment of truth for a would-be disciple. Until this point Jesus has not spoken, and we have no indication of his reaction to the woman or to the disciples. Now this becomes clear. First, Jesus reprimands his own disciples; and then he turns to the woman, and for the rest of this episode his focus is entirely on her and her astonishing and memorable act of faith and service.[5]

Jesus says, "Let her alone; why do you trouble her? She has performed a good service for me" (v. 6). He sees the distress the disciples have caused the woman, and he orders them rather sternly to desist immediately. His command indicates that they are not only interfering but actually harassing her. And those are his last words to the disciples; his full attention is given to the woman.

"She has performed a good service for me" (v. 6). Literally, she has done "a beautiful work"; this phrase resonates at a much deeper level, reaching down to the foundations of Jewish religious observance. The story of the bent-over woman concluded with the crowd—much to the officials' shame—praising "the wonderful things" Jesus was doing (see chap. 8). Now Jesus commends the woman in almost identical language,[6] so it is worth remarking that what the uneducated "crowds" in the synagogue had seen in Jesus, he in turn identifies in this action of the silent woman. He then says that "she has done what she could; she has anointed my body beforehand for its burial" (v. 7). These two phrases constitute a single sentence: he is almost certainly alluding to the "good service" or "beautiful thing" that Jews knew to refer to true religious observance. But "she has done what she could" is a phrase so easily used casually or disparagingly. Here, Jesus is using her action as exemplary. It is no casual "she did what *little* she could" but a very forceful "she has done *everything she possibly could have done*"—while the only thing the disciples have done is interfere and complain.

The verb translated here as "done" connotes an action showing mature responsibility and vision. Jesus draws attention to this, saying that she has anointed his body beforehand for its burial. But there are two other words that translate as "anoint," something that has caused much spilling of ink by scholars attempting to interpret this woman's action. What we can say is that this Markan text is a favorite when women are ordained across many of the Christian denominations, because they see her action—approved and strongly endorsed by Jesus—as a legitimate anointing: a "priestly" act. The word (*aleipho*) used in Luke's (7:38, 46) and John's (12:3) accounts is usually a festal or medical anointing or application, but it is also used for Jesus' healing acts of anointing in his hometown (Mark 6:13). The other word is *chrio*, a specifically religious rite that only ever refers to God's direct action in the New Testament. So scholars remain divided over the significance of this act. Yet Jesus seems to have no qualms: not only does he relate the anointing, specifically on the *head* (while in Luke and John the action was on the *feet*), to his impending death (as a preparatory anointing and a subsequent embalming), but he concludes with one of the most momentous and formal declarations in the entire New Testament. "Truly I tell you" hardly does justice to the weight of his concluding statement. The "Amen, amen I tell you" of the Greek, which sounds archaic in English, provides the necessary emphasis for what is coming. Jesus declares, first, that whenever the Good News (*evangelion:* gospeling) is proclaimed, *universally*, this woman and her action should be— *will be*—recounted and remembered. It is an imperative, a command or declaration: not a suggestion of recommendation.

But his "[tell this] in remembrance of her" uncannily echoes "Do this in remembrance of me" (Luke 22:19).[7] Given that he has just been anointed for his rapidly approaching death and burial, Jesus might well have said that wherever this story were told subsequently and universally, it was to be told in memory of *him*. But that is not what he said, because the person he wanted remembered was this woman of steadfast faith and courage.

It is therefore all the more regrettable that though, in Roman Catholic communities, the "sinful" woman of Luke, who washes the feet of Jesus in a servile way, is loudly proclaimed at the Sunday assembly, this holy, anonymous, exemplary woman's memory is not preserved for the edification of the community of the faithful.[8]

Recontextualization or Application

1. Do I hold back and keep a low profile? Would I ever take a risk as a sign of my commitment?

2. Do I have a deep sense of purpose, and live it by careful preparation for serious matters?

3. Do I have the faith and trust that my best efforts are good enough?

4. The woman "did [everything] she could." Do I, or am I like the disciples who murmur and criticize but do nothing?

5. Will I leave a legacy, something worth being remembered for?

10

A Sinking Feeling
(Matt 14:22-33)

[22]Immediately [Jesus] made the disciples get into the boat and go on ahead to the other side, while he dismissed the crowds. [23]And after he had dismissed the crowds, he went up the mountain by himself to pray. When evening came, he was there alone, [24]but by this time the boat, battered by the waves, was far from the land, for the wind was against them. [25]And early in the morning he came walking toward them on the sea. [26]But when the disciples saw him . . . , they were terrified, saying, "It is a ghost!" And they cried out in fear. [27]But immediately Jesus spoke to them and said, "Take heart, it is I; do not be afraid."

[28]Peter answered him, "Lord, if it is you, command me to come to you on the water." [29]He said, "Come." So Peter got out of the boat, started walking on the water, and came toward Jesus. [30]But when he noticed the strong wind, he became frightened, and beginning to sink, he cried out, "Lord, save me!" [31]Jesus immediately reached out his hand and caught him, saying to him, "You of little faith, why did you doubt?" [32]When they got into the boat, the wind ceased. [33]And those in the boat worshiped him, saying, "Truly you are the Son of God."

Part of Peter's attractiveness is surely that he is so very human. He can reach for the stars one moment and fall on his face the next, or profess his undying loyalty to Jesus and then crumple before the accusing word of a serving-girl. We look here at Peter's second call (the first is recounted in Mark 1:16-17: Peter leaves his boat and nets, to follow Jesus enthusiastically). But the second call—and there will be a third, after the resurrection, when Peter repents three times, and three times is called to "feed my lambs" and "feed my sheep" (John 21:15-17)—can serve as a reminder to all of us would-be disciples that Jesus does not simply call once and unequivocally, but that the call is reiterated in various ways throughout the lifetime of those who attempt to be attuned to the promptings of God, and who are not dispirited or destroyed by their own failures. God's love is greater than our sinfulness and God's covenant remains in force until the end of time. What is required of us, therefore, is an increase in faith and trust and a willingness to persevere. Peter is an example to all of us that we do not have to be perfect or infallible, but only persevering and faithful.

The setting for the present story is at the conclusion of the feeding of the five thousand. The *mise en scène* has Jesus, attempting to be alone for a while, being pursued by a vast crowd—ironically, one of his most favored situations. The crowd (*ochlos*) is the motley group of people not distinguished by privilege or education, but attracted to Jesus for a variety of worthy and less worthy motives. In this case, Matthew says they had *heard* about Jesus' whereabouts (a preamble to discipleship itself) and draws an interesting contrast between the eager crowds and the less-than-receptive disciples. Jesus speaks to the crowds, shows compassion, and heals their sick (Matt 14:14), unlike the Twelve whose pastoral response is "send the crowds away" so that they can "buy food for themselves" (14:15). But Jesus challenges them, saying, "you give them something to eat" (14:16). We know the rest: how impotent the disciples appear and how the creativity of Jesus astounds everyone.

Our story begins at this point. Jesus continues to seek solitude for contemplation,[1] something that is quite beyond the disciples at this stage. So he needs to separate himself from them, and he does indeed "dismiss" the crowds now that they have been nourished (the verb is the same one the disciples had used in asking that Jesus "dismiss" the crowds in a significantly less compassionate way). Jesus gives the Twelve a very simple task: to row across the lake, where he will join them at an unspecified time. This should not have been too taxing, though the lake was notoriously unpredictable. But they were proud fishermen, though they could be far too self-assured at times. Nevertheless, they should not be daunted by an evening trip on the lake they knew well enough. Matthew's text speaks not of the lake but of "the sea," and not simply of a boat but a "ship" being "tossed" or "buffeted": a little hyperbole makes the story more effective. Verse 24 is interesting: in English it reads "the wind was against/contrary/in opposition to"—but whether to the boat or to the sailors is not specified. But "the wind" can symbolize the Holy Spirit; and people sometimes act in opposition or contrary to the Spirit. In any case, the wind or Spirit is much stronger, and those who do not adjust and stop fighting the Spirit's prevailing wind risk being overwhelmed and swamped. The end of the story seems to complete this thought, as we will see.

Matthew says it was "the fourth watch of the night" or "first light," a little before dawn when one could just distinguish the horizon—or a person. The Greek is very specific: the disciples' immediate reaction was to be agitated or "disturbed." Like a chorus, they shout out together, "It is a ghost"—literally, "a phantasm" or apparition (v. 26). Insofar as we can identify a disturbance as one of three critical stages on the way to discipleship,[2] a disturbance is exactly what the Twelve are experiencing now—not for the first or the last time—and it occurs prior to this particular call and encounter with Jesus.

Even though they have only recently left Jesus, it is not entirely surprising that this was the disciples' first reaction: it was still semi-dark; their culture and its people were prone to superstition; and the appearance of a person actually walking on the water was not something the rational mind could easily comprehend. But "they cried out in fear"—and this time they are not just disturbed but terrified. There is no braggadocio, no bravura, but only raw human vulnerability. "But immediately Jesus spoke," says Matthew, borrowing Mark's effective device ("immediately") for linking two sentences or events; there is no hesitation, and the voice should convince them that it is not a phantom.

We recall that, after the resurrection, nobody seems to recognize Jesus in his bodily form, but they do recognize his voice. In Matthew's account, Mary Magdalene and the other Mary (Matt 28:9) do so. In Luke, the two en route to Emmaus recognized him in action—"in the breaking of the bread" (Luke 24:31). Yet even after the Emmaus episode, when the disciples seem to have identified the risen Christ, still, when he appeared once more, "They thought they were seeing a ghost" (Luke 24:37). In John's account, Mary Magdalene thought at first that she was encountering the gardener, but then recognized Jesus by his voice (John 20:15). Clearly, the risen Christ is not immediately physically recognizable, but even earlier the disciples were as likely to think they were seeing a ghost walking on the water as to recognize Jesus in the present circumstances, either by sight or by hearing.

On this occasion Jesus says three things: "Take heart; It is I; do not be afraid" (v. 27). In this text, the verb for "take heart" or "have courage" is exactly the word the disciples themselves used to address Bartimaeus rather condescendingly and after they had tried to silence him—an action rather similar to their desire to send the hungry crowd away. Is Jesus gently reminding them of their condescension on that occasion? In this case, though, he is also genuinely giving them a reason for courage: the fact that it is indeed him—he says, "It is I."

If someone knocks on your door, and in answer to your "who is it?" that person says simply, "it's me," the assumption is that the two have recently spoken and that the two persons know each other and recognize their respective voices. Jesus assumed the same on this occasion. But there is of course much more here, since the formal "IT IS I" (the *ego eimi* or "I am Who [I] am") are classic words Jesus uses to reveal his full identity at very significant moments, as the God of the Hebrew Bible did since the ancient days. Of course the disciples may not realize this at the time, but decades later Matthew's community, with this text in their hands or ringing in their ears, would certainly be aware of the weight of these words of Jesus. His third statement is "be not afraid"—which of course is precisely what they are at this moment! It is widely, but erroneously, thought that "be not afraid" occurs 365 times in the Bible: conveniently one for each day of the year. But it does occur more than one hundred times, indicating that being afraid is a very common human condition. These disciples certainly knew fear at that moment, but the words of Jesus are the very encouragement they need.

Given the circumstances, Peter's response is almost laughable: "*if it is you*" (v. 28), he says, and then, immediately, impulsively, imperiously, and dramatically, "command me to come to you on the water." Sometimes we get exactly what we ask for, and Peter's request would get him into deep water, because the very next word from the mouth of Jesus was a simple, "Come!" This is once more an explicit and urgent call, and Peter has asked for it, literally. And yet Peter—spokesperson, if not leader, of the Twelve—cannot afford to lose face in this impossible situation at this critical moment. He had prefaced his calls with "Lord," a formal and respectful term of address; but as yet it is not an effective indication that he really has faith in Jesus. And faith, of course, is exactly what Jesus is looking for. Jesus has just said, "Come": in other words, "Trust me; take the leap (of faith)." And to his enormous credit, that is exactly what Peter does, instantly, and probably without thinking. While the rest of the disciples hunker down in the boat, terrified (as most of us would be), Peter clambers over the gunwale, starts walking on the water, "and [comes] toward Jesus" (v. 29). He is definitely heading in the right direction, and his intentions are good: he is coming "toward" Jesus; but he is not there yet. These steps are, truly, his walk in faith; and he falters.

As long as his eyes were fixed on Jesus, he would be enabled to do the impossible, but the moment he became self-conscious and fully aware of what was happening, he became totally disoriented, like a tightrope walker who looks down, loses his balance, and begins to fall. Peter now became conscious of the strong wind that had already threatened to wreck the boat, the wind that was contrary and potentially lethal, and he knew his position was unsustainable. Although Jesus has told him not to be afraid, he could not help himself and, inevitably, began to sink. But in the very moment of his awareness that he was sinking, "he cried out, 'Lord, save me!'" No longer is this the tentative "Lord, *if* it is you"; this is now the certainty of one who knows his only hope. "Lord, save" is as close to an act of real faith that Peter can muster in this terrifying moment. This is not faith in the afterlife or notional faith in the unseen God: Peter simply believes that Jesus—and only Jesus—can save him from imminent drowning. Again, Matthew links Peter's request with Jesus' response: "Jesus immediately reached out his hand and caught him" (v. 31). This is another example of the sheer human physicality of Jesus; as he embraced the woman in the synagogue who had been deprived of demonstrations of human affect for so long, so now he hugs and hauls Peter, giving him the physical assurance that he is now safe in the embrace of his "Lord." But even before they get back in the boat, Jesus gives him another lesson about discipleship: "You of little faith, why did you doubt?" (v. 31). The verb implies having second thoughts, being ambivalent. What Peter needed was stead-fastness, not fickle faith; little faith is just not good enough for a true disciple.

The story is beautifully rounded out by yet another reference to the wind: previously wild and contrary, it has now abated. If it is Matthew's way of showing the opposition between the disciples and the Spirit of God, now there is no such opposition. Jesus is with them in the boat; there is no further contrariness; harmony has returned. But one striking image concludes this dramatic episode, and it is pure Matthew, always ready to support the disciples' falter-ing faith and cover their most obvious weaknesses. The disciples, he says, having been challenged, chastised, and chastened, finally believe: they "worshiped him, saying, 'Truly you are the Son of God'" (v. 33). It is a story for the ages, a "happily-ever-after" story, though there will be many more doubts, second thoughts, and even betrayals. "The Way" of Jesus and the way of discipleship are not easy to negotiate. Mark's conclusion to this episode is much, much darker, as we may note (Mark 6:51-52).[3]

Matthew's account has shown Peter's four steps to faith. First he addressed Jesus as a ghost. Then he became a little more courageous, calling him "Lord"—but conditionally; he says "Lord, *if it is you.*" From there he becomes decidedly firmer and more committed, crying out with conviction, a third time, "Lord, save me!" Now there is no conditional "if," but only a deep-seated plea for help from the one he knows is there. And finally, he, accompanied by the chorus of voices of the rest of the apostles, professes their communal faith: "Truly you are the Son of God."

Recontextualization or Application

1. Am I struggling "against the wind" of God's Spirit and beginning to panic?

2. What is it that makes me so afraid?

3. Do I always follow my instincts to "stay in the boat" and hunker down during crises?

4. At this point in my life, do I *dare* to ask again for the call of Jesus?

5. Do I have the steadfast faith to get out of the boat, come what may?

11

A Father's Faith
and a Woman's Endurance
(Mark 5:21-43)

Overview

Mark has constructed another gem of a story with many telling details about how people's faith develops and matures and thus brings them to the verge of discipleship. The structure of this narrative makes it an intercalation: like a letter inside an envelope, the envelope itself is the story of Jairus, while that of the suffering woman is inserted like a letter within. But Mark makes some telling connections between the two stories. We will take the passage in three sections: the opening of the story of Jairus's daughter; the whole of the story of the bleeding woman; and, finally, the conclusion to the Jairus story.

Jairus and His Daughter (vv. 21-24)

[21]When Jesus had crossed again in the boat to the other side, a great crowd gathered around him; and he was by the sea. [22]Then one of the leaders of the synagogue named Jairus came and, when he saw him, fell at his feet [23]and begged him repeatedly, "My little daughter is at the point of death. Come and lay your hands on her, so that she may be made well, and live." [24]So he went with him. And a large crowd followed him and pressed in on him.

116

Jesus has just come from the land of the Gerasenes[1] and now returns to the Jewish side of the lake or Sea of Galilee where he had called the first disciples. They are back on home territory again. This is simply another example of the peripatetic boundary-crossing ministry of Jesus who, though always on "the Way" to Jerusalem, will continually go *out of his way* to find people who have *lost their way* or fallen *by the wayside*—like the demoniac of Gerasa who was actually living in the cemetery or the tombs, and who "begged that he might be with" Jesus. Having first been healed, he was then commissioned as a disciple and sent to the cities of the Decapolis (5:19-20). And now, as so often happened, "a great crowd" (*ochlos*[2]) followed, as well as the inner group of the Twelve.

Out of nowhere, Jairus—a senior religious leader and man of some social prominence—runs up, abandons his dignity, and in great distress seems to throw himself right at the feet of Jesus, rather like the rich man would do later (Mark 10:17). This again is a sign of acknowledgment, respect, urgency, and petitioning—if not at this point a gesture of worship born of faith in Jesus. The urgency is evident from his repeated begging on behalf of his mortally ill daughter. The impending (biological) death of the child will be a contrast to actual social death of the woman in the later part of the story. Jairus does not address Jesus, either by name or by title, but as he pours out his brief and sorry tale there is unquestionably a sign that he has faith. He begs Jesus to lay his hands on her, a request that might be considered to indicate some expectation of a quasi-magical healing. But he adds, significantly, one of three *divine passives* in this narrative. "So that she may *be made well*" indicates his conviction that God is involved in the healing touch of Jesus. Jesus is no magician or charlatan. But his response—from the one who normally asks other people to follow him—is to follow Jairus to his home: an indication of his willingness literally to go out of his way to help. It also illustrates his own teaching that the first should become the last and that he himself had come to serve (see Mark 10:44-45). The large crowd, already mentioned, follows in hot pursuit.

Before we continue with that story, however, the second story now unfolds in its entirety.

The Bleeding Woman (vv. 25-34)

[25]Now there was a woman who had been suffering from hemorrhages for twelve years. [26]She had endured much under many physicians, and had spent all that she had; and she was no better, but rather grew worse. [27]She had heard about Jesus, and came up behind him in the crowd and touched his cloak, [28]for she said, "If I but touch his clothes, I will be made well." [29]Immediately her hemorrhage stopped; and she felt in her body that she was healed of her disease. [30]Immediately aware that power had gone forth from him, Jesus turned about in the crowd and said, "Who touched my clothes?" [31]And his disciples said to him, "You see the crowd pressing in on you; how can you say, 'Who touched me?'" [32]He looked all around to see who had done it. [33]But the woman, knowing what had happened to her, came in fear and trembling, fell down before him, and told him the whole truth. [34]He said to her, "Daughter, your faith has made you well; go in peace, and be healed of your disease."

This story opens with, "There was a woman." The bent-over woman (Luke 13:10) whom we met earlier (see chap. 8) was described as profoundly present ("a woman *was* [there]," italics added), deeply committed to being in the synagogue. Not so this woman, who is introduced rather generically, simply as "a certain woman." But if the life expectancy was only around thirty years or so, and she has been suffering the social death of ritually unclean bleeding for twelve years, those facts indicate a condition that started as early as her first menstruation.[3] Like the bent woman, her adult life too has been thoroughly compromised, and with it her chance of marriage, family, and physical displays of human affection. She has been socially dead since she became socially alive: in other words, since she became a woman, and the general populace will feel revulsion since this was the kind of sickness that marked her as contaminated and ritually infectious.

To add to her plight, she had suffered from the very physicians she hoped would help her, becoming a virtual beggar in the process. This is yet another example of how the institution (not, this time, the synagogue leaders we saw in chapter 8, or the Twelve we met in the following chapter, but this time the medical professionals) can get in the way and come between Jesus and a person seeking help. There remains a constant danger that social institutions that should be assisting people—including the church—can be obstacles that do precisely the opposite. In consulting physicians, in fact, the woman's condition had actually worsened (v. 26).[4]

However, in this case the Jewish people had been expressly warned not to consult physicians but to put their trust in God alone.[5] Perhaps the woman has failed to observe religious rules in this respect, and in her distress she is turning to Jesus as a last resort? Not so, for the text is clear. First, "she had *heard* about Jesus," and hearing is the preamble to a faith response. And she articulates her own faith using yet another *divine passive*: she believes that as long as she can touch Jesus, God will respond. She does not believe in magic but, having heard, she acts: she approaches Jesus within the anonymity of the crowd, but from behind. She does not want to be noticed because of the crowd's possible adverse reaction. She is, after all, someone who should not be out in public.

But Jesus, of course, spends a significant part of his public life encountering and embracing precisely the pariahs—lepers, adulterers,[6] and sinners in general—in order to exhibit what has been called "reverse contamination." He identifies some of the current thinking as bad theology, as if to say that God does not condemn these people as "contaminated," but that if there is to be any "appropriate" contamination, it will be that of the effect of his contact on everyone: truly "Godly contamination"![7]

Mark's signature word, "immediately," recurs in this story. First, the instant the woman touched the cloak of Jesus, her bleeding stopped. Then, "immediately" aware, Jesus reacted. When Jesus heals or performs a work of power,[8] he feels depleted—one reason that he consistently chooses to remove himself for contemplative prayer, union with his *Abba*, and personal restoration or replenishment after an arduous day. Even though the woman only touched his cloak, he felt the effect, while the woman herself sensed beforehand that this would be sufficient to trigger his healing powers. But Jesus' reaction—as with much of the rationale for his ministry and its effects—is lost on the Twelve when he says, "who touched my clothes?" (v. 30). They can only state the obvious: there is a great crowd around, so Jesus should not be surprised if he is jostled anonymously. But of course—like the woman—Jesus knows better. As he turns to identify whoever touched him, she takes the initiative, coming toward Jesus "in fear and trembling." She is *coming to Jesus*, seeking the encounter she had been avoiding heretofore: another promising indication of discipleship. But why the fear? Apart from the simple fact that she would be singled out in a large crowd—something that would make her self-conscious—she was, one can easily imagine, afraid, not of Jesus, but of the crowd itself: if someone in the crowd realized her condition, the crowd could very easily turn into a mob and trample her to death. She is at very serious risk in this moment.

In a single movement, the woman throws herself at the feet of Jesus (the same verb-root is used for Jairus's gesture of real respect and urgency), "and told him the whole truth" (v. 33). This is precisely what impresses Jesus: truth-telling. He affirms the same thing in the woman at the well (John 4:18), as he proceeds to draw her into a deep theological discussion, completely uninterested in her sexual history. So this distressed woman pours out her soul to Jesus, telling him everything: the embarrassing and intimate nature of her ailment, her penury as a result of trusting physicians, and her deteriorating physical—and presumably mental—state (v. 26). The response of Jesus was immediate: "Daughter, your faith has made you well; go in peace, and be healed of your disease" (v. 34). With the same word he used to dignify the bent woman, Jesus now calls this anonymous woman, too, a "daughter (of Abraham)":[9] she is loved by God as one of the chosen people, morally equal to all those "sons of Abraham" who habitually ignore or marginalize her. It is unlikely that Jesus is simply calling her "daughter" as a term of affection used by a man old enough to be her father. She may indeed be a little younger than Jesus, but not by much, and a theological allusion seems more appropriate in these circumstances, since he immediately identifies her faith as the enabling cause of her healing. Faith makes miracles: miracles rarely make faith. And here, very evidently, is a woman of faith. Jesus has not "laid hands" on her but does declare that her healing has *already* taken place ("your faith *has made you well*").

In this story we have all three stages of discipleship. First, the encounter; then the disturbance; and now the sending forth: "Go," says Jesus, "and be healed of your disease"—another *divine passive*, acknowledging the direct action of God. So she is sent forth, commissioned by Jesus to tell of God's mighty works. An interesting feature of this encounter is that Jesus never asked her exactly what was wrong or what she wanted. And although "she told him the whole truth" (v. 33), we are not made privy to any of her actual words! This is often the case with the women disciples: their faith is in their actions rather than their words. And so we in turn, are left impressed by her courage, her integrity, and her fierce faith.

Jairus and His Daughter (vv. 35-43)

[35]While he was still speaking, some people came from the leader's house to say, "Your daughter is dead. Why trouble the teacher any further?" [36]But overhearing what they said, Jesus said to the leader of the synagogue, "Do not fear, only believe." [37]He allowed no one to follow him except Peter, James, and John, the brother of James. [38]When they came to the house of the leader of the synagogue, he saw a commotion, people weeping and wailing loudly. [39]When he had entered, he said to them, "Why do you make a commotion and weep? The child is not dead but sleeping." [40]And they laughed at him. Then he put them all outside, and took the child's father and mother and those who were with him, and went in where the child was. [41]He took her by the hand and said to her, "Talitha cum," which means, "Little girl, get up!" [42]And immediately the girl got up and began to walk about (she was twelve years of age). At this they were overcome

with amazement. [43]He strictly ordered them that no one should know this, and told them to give her something to eat.

Without further preamble we now return to the story of Jairus's daughter. Mark makes the transition with a neat turn: from concluding Jesus' interaction with the woman whom he calls "daughter," Mark now puts the very same word on the lips of the messengers from Jairus's house. "Your daughter is dead" (v. 35), they say, thus linking the woman and the girl. The woman had just moved from (social) death to life, while the girl had by now moved from (biological) life to death. And at the end of the story, the two will be linked again by Mark's insightful comment. Meanwhile, Jesus, who consistently calls others to follow him, is still following Jairus to his house, when some people arrive from the house and starkly announce the girl's death to the devastated father. It would seem from the narrative that Jairus had witnessed the interaction between Jesus and the bleeding woman, and he must have been getting increasingly agitated about his daughter. But now, it seems, it is too late; Jesus had been delayed by the woman, and now Jairus's daughter is dead. But Jesus, who calls other people to use their ears to listen, hear, and act, is also listening now, and he overhears the message. Turning to Jairus he says what he repeats so often, "Do not fear, only believe." Jairus has just witnessed the power of the woman's faith and Jesus' response. Now, at least, Jesus is side by side with Jairus, even though it does seem much too late to "only believe." Jairus knows a dead person when he sees one.

At this point Jesus manages to put some distance between himself and the crowds, taking only his three closest disciples—Peter, James, and John—and following Jairus to his home. The funeral rites were already in full swing, with people keening and wailing, perhaps ululating, and generally making a great deal of noise in the courtyard of Jairus's house. The verb Mark uses can apply to a civil disturbance or clamor, but here it refers to a formal, choreographed, and yet semi-spontaneous ritual of lamentation. Jesus appears to indicate that such lamentation is premature, because "the child is not dead but sleeping" (v. 39). His words fall on deaf ears: they know a dead body when they see one (though not everyone would have been able actually to see the child in her small room). Most people believe what others tell them. The text says they laughed at, or ridiculed, Jesus, but their reaction might well have been a touch hysterical (the crowd by now is in full lamentation mode and highly aroused emotionally) as much as a personal reflection on Jesus. In any event, as he had distanced himself from the crowds, he now does the same with the mourners. Making space for himself and his three disciples, Jesus enters the confines of the girl's room, but taking the girl's parents too. He has created a little community, as witnesses, as support for the parents, and, in a moment, as familiar faces that the little girl will immediately recognize.

Taking the initiative, Jesus reaches out to the dead yet still warm body—quite unafraid of the contamination associated with a corpse—and holds her hand, a universal gesture of tenderness, presence, and communication. Quietly and gently, he speaks into her ear the kinds of words she would have heard from her loving parents: almost baby language, and certainly profoundly affectionate, not a literal "little girl," but something like a very appropriate and affectionate paternal "sweetheart" or "darling" to our ears. We will no longer be surprised that the next word is, again, "immediately" (v. 42). No sooner does Jesus gently call her, than she responded. And it is at this point that, in telling us that she was not so little (she was perfectly capable of walking), Mark links her story with the previous one, saying, "she was twelve years of age." She is a girl who, after twelve years of life as a child (a social nobody) but now at the age of menarche and on the verge of womanhood and marriage, is about to begin the new life of an adult woman and mother—a life that was actually cut short, until Jesus restored it (which was exactly what he came to do: to restore the people of Israel). This story is in touching contrast to that of the virtual nonperson, the hemorrhaging woman who has been a social nobody for twelve years. Now she too, healed of something like chronic dysmenorrhea, is restored from (social) death to the social and domestic life of an adult woman.

Not surprisingly, the parents—and, not for the first time, the three apostles—were "struck with amazement" (v. 42). And not for the last time would Jesus try, in vain, to keep the "messianic secret" by not drawing attention to himself, by attempting to deter the merely curious or novelty seekers, and by deferring his healing acts to the power of his *Abba*.

The final phrase—he "told them to give her something to eat"—will perhaps come back to Peter, James, and John a little later. When Jesus asks them to respond to the needs of the crowd of five thousand (maybe seventeen thousand or more if the women and children were counted), as he had done to the daughter of Jairus and the bleeding woman, their best pastoral suggestion is that he should send them away to buy their own food! How quickly they had forgotten that Jesus, considerate of the girl's appetite, told her parents (and themselves) to give her something to eat (v. 43) as he would tell them, "You give them something to eat [yourselves]" (Mark 6:37). Amazement itself does not make a disciple; but compassion, imagination, and foresight do go a long way in the right direction: the Way of Jesus.

Recontextualization or Application

1. Like Jairus, do I truly care about anyone more than myself?

2. Like the woman, am I persistent and faithful in seeking deep healing?

3. The woman "told him the whole truth." Dare I tell my whole truth to anyone?

4. Often Jesus says, "Do not fear, only believe." Is my faith as strong as my fear?

5. "They were overcome with amazement." Am I still open to being amazed by God, perhaps evident through the needs of another person?

12

An Unfinished Symphony
(John 4:3-42)

Overview

The story of the encounter between Jesus and a Samaritan woman is one of the most dramatic—and the longest—in the New Testament. This chapter will explore her call to discipleship and mission, but in three stages, rather like three movements of a symphony. But, as with the other New Testament encounters, the story as recounted by John is not the end of the story. The woman is starting a new life as a disciple, and each of us, in turn, is invited to respond to these biblical stories by reviewing our own lives in their light and recommitting ourselves to following "the Way" of Jesus. This chapter is titled "unfinished symphony" as a reminder that we still have a long way to go in our own efforts to follow the Way.

First Movement: "Living Water and Eternal Life" (vv. 3-15)

³[Jesus] left Judea and started back to Galilee. ⁴But he had to go through Samaria. ⁵So he came to a Samaritan city called Sychar, near the plot of ground that Jacob had given to his son Joseph. ⁶Jacob's well was there, and Jesus, tired out by his journey, was sitting by the well. It was about noon.

⁷A Samaritan woman came to draw water, and Jesus said to her, "Give me a drink." ⁸(His disciples had gone to the city to buy food.)

> ⁹The Samaritan woman said to him, "How is it that you, a Jew, ask a drink of me, a woman of Samaria?" (Jews do not share things in common with Samaritans.) ¹⁰Jesus answered her, "If you knew the gift of God, and who it is that is saying to you, 'Give me a drink,' you would have asked him, and he would have given you living water." ¹¹The woman said to him, "Sir, you have no bucket, and the well is deep. Where do you get that living water? ¹²Are you greater than our ancestor Jacob, who gave us the well, and with his sons and his flocks drank from it?" ¹³Jesus said to her, "Everyone who drinks of this water will be thirsty again, ¹⁴but those who drink of the water that I will give them will never be thirsty. The water that I will give will become in them a spring of water gushing up to eternal life." ¹⁵The woman said to him, "Sir, give me this water, so that I may never be thirsty or have to keep coming here to draw water."

The root of the Hebrew word for conversion is -*shub*, and its first meaning is "to go back home." According to many Jewish people today, the story of the Prodigal Son (Luke 15:11-24) is one of the most "Jewish" stories of the New Testament and is, of course, the story of a man who leaves home and all it stands for, only to return home later as a much-changed person, astonished in discovering his father's abiding love. The story of the Samaritan woman is similarly a story of a woman who leaves home to draw water on a very ordinary day, only to return home later a thoroughly changed and converted disciple. This story also has all three elements or stages of discipleship: an encounter, a disturbance, and a sending forth or co-missioning by Jesus.

The text says that it was necessary for Jesus to pass through Samaria on the way back to Galilee from Judea. However, the route through Samaria was not the only possibility, and some scholars see the "had to" (v. 4) as providentially rather than absolutely necessary: Jesus *had to* go out of his way in order to call people to the Way, and that included Samaritans; after all, that was his mission. The Samaritans—who survive to this day near Nablus, Palestine, some thirty miles north of Jerusalem—were an established group within Judaism that worshiped on Mount Gerizim and were thus in a polemical relationship with those who worshiped in Jerusalem.[1] Some Jewish leaders regarded them as apostates (2 Kgs 17:24-34). Jacob's well is, technically, a cistern: a reservoir rather than a spring. The water does not flow like a stream or gush like a fountainhead, but appears as still—rather than running—water. This is extremely significant for anyone who wants to understand the conversation between Jesus and the woman.

As mentioned earlier, John's gospel is famous for its high Christology, in which Jesus seems to know everything all the time. All the more striking, then, that this text states explicitly that "Jesus, tired out by his journey, was sitting by [Jacob's] well" (v. 6), when a Samaritan woman came to draw water. As soon as she encounters him, the woman is in the superior position—unless he stands up (and is taller than she), which he evidently does not.[2] To ignore him is probably her best reaction under the circumstances. So she must be deeply shocked when he addresses her but without moving from his seated position. A Jewish man (especially a teacher or rabbi) speaking to a Samaritan woman in public—especially if he initiated the conversation—was regarded as scandalous. Moreover, he must be looking up to her as she, perforce, looks down on him. But Jesus is ostensibly the social superior, and she the inferior. He is a Jew, and (from a Jewish perspective) she is a heretical Samaritan. He is a man, and she a mere woman. And yet he is the needy one at this point, and she is very much in control of the situation. Nevertheless, the thirsty would-be recipient opens the interaction by appearing to demand (rather rudely) of his would-be donor, "Give me a drink" (v. 7), and nothing (such as "please" or "excuse me") softens the imperiousness of these few words. It is a strange scene: a Samaritan woman, alone and in a public place in the middle of the day; a stranger, and a Jewish man at that, addressing her from an inferior position; and an unsubtle and potentially offensive request. And yet it sets in motion a series of exchanges that become increasingly theological in tone. From the outset, Jesus seems to be intentionally obtuse and unconventional.

The evangelist interjects several asides in order to tighten the focus between Jesus and the woman, and also for a later audience —contemporaries of Jesus would have understood as self-evident that Jews and Samaritans were not friendly (v. 9). The first of these (v. 8) nicely removes the Twelve from the scene. The woman reacts to Jesus' question by showing that she is quite aware of the unconventional nature of this encounter; but she also stands up to him: she does not immediately offer to give him the drink he demands (in fact he may never have received a drink at all). We do not always get exactly what we ask or bargain for. Having asked and failed to receive, Jesus then speaks what can only be an incomprehensible statement: "If you knew the gift of God, and who it is that is saying to you, 'Give me a drink,' you would have asked him, and he would have given you living water" (v. 10). Read for the first time, each phrase is meaningless, and the whole statement seems deliberately obtuse and contrary.

But consider four points. First, if we add the word "only" to the opening phrase, some of Jesus' urgency becomes more apparent: "If *only* you knew." He does not simply wish that she knew; he *wants* her to know his identity, as will soon be very apparent. Second, "the gift of God" can easily be understood as a gift that God wishes to give her—as one person would give a memento to another. But this is quite different: the gift *is* God. The meaning here is that the "God-gift" is both gift and giver, and that Jesus wants the woman to receive it. This notion is intrinsically quite amazing, and even more shocking under the circumstances: the gift is to be offered to this particular woman, unworthy in so many ways. The disciples are nowhere to be seen, having gone to the city "to buy food" (v. 8), a detail that clearly indicates their priorities in Samaritan territory or perhaps that Jesus had deliberately sent them away.

Third, "if *only* you knew who it is that is [speaking] to you." Jesus presents himself as an anonymous, Jewish, Galilean stranger, so how could she possibly know his identity? He is certainly not making things easy for her. But, fourth, he says that "he would have given you living water." (He does not use the first person "I.") This is not "the

water of life," which might have been understood as something alco-
holic or medicinal, but literally "water-living" (or "living water"),
which she, quite understandably, has never heard of. Perhaps she
thinks he means "flowing" in contrast to the water in the cistern: at
least then she would not have needed to plunge a bucket down into
the well, but might have allowed the water to flow into her bucket or
water jar. Yet for some reason she neither dismisses his apparent wanderings nor excuses herself: she chooses a line of conversation that
becomes increasingly and surprisingly theological and nuanced.

Adopting a distinctly respectful form of address, she calls him sir
(*kurios*, lord), yet her tone seems condescending or even lightly mock-
ing: she knows she has the upper hand and that his promise of water
(as she understands it) is impossible to fulfill. "You have no bucket,
and the well is deep. Where do you get that living water?" There is
almost a "who do you think you are?" in her next reference, to Jacob
the eponymous donor of the well (v. 12). To which Jesus responds—
first with a statement of the obvious but then with another impenetrable statement and a personal promise—the well water is natural
and unexceptional, but the promise of Jesus is of something unimaginable, completely and indefinitely lasting thirst-quenching water.

A moment before, Jesus referred to himself obliquely, not in the
first person but as "he." Now he speaks in an explicitly personal way
of "the water that I will give" (v. 14). And he makes two promises:
first, of spring water, and second, mysteriously, of "eternal life." She
knows what the first entails, but has only a rudimentary idea of the
second, as relating to life after death. But he is not speaking simply
of a spring as distinct from a well. And the "eternal life" to which
he refers is both something that does not happen only after death
but here and now: it gushes, spouts, pours forth in a surge of qualitatively new life, which is inconceivable to the woman. A hard-
headed pragmatist, she immediately jumps to the wrong conclusion:
he is offering some kind of labor-saving device, a quick and easy
way to obtain plentiful water. "Sir," she says again, "give me this
water, so that I may never be thirsty again or have to keep coming
here to draw water" (v. 15).

Evidently Jesus and the woman are talking at cross-purposes: she is speaking of her routine, mundane concerns, and he is talking about present and eternal possibilities. He has neither identified nor explained himself, yet he has promised something she cannot possibly understand. She, for her part, has neither dismissed him as a madman nor communicated with him in a meaningful way. But she has taken one significant step toward faith in Jesus the stranger. From initially addressing him as "Sir" (as did Bartimaeus) but with a degree of aloofness or hostility, she now addresses him, still as "Sir" but now with an added request: "give me this water," a sign that she wants to pursue the conversation and make some sense out of this odd encounter. The first movement of this unfolding symphony closes on a discordant note: harmony and dialogue remain elusive.

Recontextualization or Application

1. Jesus "had to go" through Samaria. What "must" I do in order to be a faithful boundary-crossing disciple? To what boundaries does God providentially call me?

2. "Give me a drink," says Jesus. What does Jesus ask of me at this time?

3. "If only you knew the God-gift," says Jesus. What is God's gift to me, and in how many ways is it apparent to me? Do I show appropriate gratitude?

4. What keeps me busy, coming and going, day after day? Am I in a rut (which South African missiologist Davis Bosch described as "a shallow grave")?

5. People ask for a drink in many ways. How do I respond to unexpected—and repeated—requests? How do I make excuses or justify my lack of sensitivity?

Second Movement: "God-Gift"—A Stranger's Identity (vv. 16-27)

¹⁶Jesus said to her, "Go, call your husband, and come back." ¹⁷The woman answered him, "I have no husband." Jesus said to her, "You are right in saying, 'I have no husband'; ¹⁸for you have had five husbands, and the one you have now is not your husband. What you have said is true!" ¹⁹The woman said to him, "Sir, I see that you are a prophet. ²⁰Our ancestors worshiped on this mountain, but you say that the place where people must worship is in Jerusalem." ²¹Jesus said to her, "Woman, believe me, the hour is coming when you will worship the Father neither on this mountain nor in Jerusalem. ²²You worship what you do not know; we worship what we know, for salvation is from the Jews. ²³But the hour is coming, and is now here, when the true worshipers will worship the Father in spirit and truth, for the Father seeks such as these to worship him. ²⁴God is spirit, and those who worship him must worship in spirit and truth." ²⁵The woman said to him, "I know that Messiah is coming" (who is called Christ). "When he comes, he will proclaim all things to us." ²⁶Jesus said to her, "I am he, the one who is speaking to you."

²⁷Just then his disciples came. They were astonished that he was speaking with a woman, but no one said, "What do you want?" or, "Why are you speaking with her?"

The second movement begins with a little wordplay between the stranger and the woman at the well. The Greek word *anēr* means simply "man" but also, where appropriate, "husband," just as the word *gunē* means "woman" or "wife." A male person is expected to grow up to be a man and a husband too, while a female is expected to mature into a woman and a wife: the one word does duty for the two social identities. In the next exchange, the distinction is critical if the full meaning is to be brought out. Here it is: Jesus said, "Go, call your *husband*." The woman answered, "I have no *husband*." But the next sentence should read: Jesus said, "You are right in saying, 'I have no *husband*'; for you have had five [*men*], and the [*man*] you have now is not your *husband*." The Samaritan is not a serial monogamist but a promiscuous woman. And yet this is much less a judgment on the part of Jesus than it is a commendation: Jesus is not interested in judging her sexual history, but only in identifying her integrity through her truth-telling. She has been promiscuous but she is not a liar, and he affirms that twice (vv. 17, 18).

She may have been surprised at Jesus' insight into her sexual history, but she is even more impressed by his personal stature: "Sir, I see that you are a prophet," she says. From an unpromising "You, a Jew," through "Sir" and an observation, she has moved to "Sir" and a question ("give me"), and now identifies Jesus as "Sir" and "a prophet": in four increments, she has moved in exactly the direction Jesus is seeking—toward faith in Jesus. She is not quite there yet, but even his own closest disciples have not yet been able to identify Jesus in this way. Having intimated that Jesus is likely a prophet, she continues to show her theological knowledge and even sophistication, identifying one of the key bones of contention between Jews and Samaritans: the appropriate place for worship. For Samaritans it is Mount Gerizim, but for Jews it is the Jerusalem temple.

"Woman, believe me," says Jesus, addressing her in the vocative case ("O, woman") and explicitly indicating the respect he had not shown her at their first interaction ("Give me a drink"). Showing her respect as a Samaritan and a woman, he is now inviting her to put her faith in him, the Jewish stranger. This is the second stage of discipleship: after the initial *encounter* (stage 1), there now follows the *disturbance* or *displacement*: the test of her willingness to follow Jesus. It is a real disturbance in view of the verses that follow (vv. 21-24), which we contemporary readers need to understand in our own theological and social context.

"The hour is coming when you will worship the Father neither on this mountain nor in Jerusalem" (v. 21) is a shocking and revolutionary statement, implying that she is able to worship authentically, but that neither of their respective holy sites is absolutely necessary. Jesus will explain this in verses 23-24. But verse 22 is hugely problematic: Jesus suddenly appears to turn from commendation to confrontation and from dialogue to rigid judgment. But first, if we were simply to omit verse 22, the text would read seam-

lessly: "The hour is coming when you [plural] will worship the
Father neither on this mountain nor in Jerusalem. . . . [T]he hour
is . . . now here when true worshipers will worship the Father in
spirit and truth, for the Father seeks such as these to worship him."
Far from judgmental, this is extremely encouraging, visionary, and
inclusive of the woman. Moreover, the hour is now—and Jesus had
just told the woman about "living water" springing up for eternal
life here and now (v. 15). So what are we to make of verse 22?

By the time this gospel came to be written—long after the destruction of Jerusalem and its temple in 70 CE—relations between Jews
and Samaritans had soured even more. The Christian community
was very much on the defensive, and this passage appears to have
been edited with the late addition of verse 22. But as we see if we
omit it, the discourse between Jesus and the woman develops much
more naturally and persuasively. When verse 22 is interpolated,
though, the whole tenor of the passage turns sour. Perhaps if we
place parentheses around that verse, we are much closer to the Good
News of Jesus.

Still on a positive note, then, the woman is paying serious attention to Jesus but she is no sponge: she knows something about her
own tradition. So she states clearly, "I *know* that Messiah is coming
(who is called Christ)." Although she had not known (for how could
she?) the "God-gift" (the "gift of God" in v. 10), now she affirms
what she does know: not only that the Messiah would come, but
that "when he comes he will proclaim all things to us" (v. 25). She
may well not be a woman of strict religious observance, but she is
showing that she is a woman of honest and deep belief, now verging
on real faith in Jesus. Astonishingly, in the absence of his Twelve
closest disciples (who had gone for lunch) and far from his home
or from Jerusalem, but in the territory of the Samaritans and in the
presence of a woman with a certain reputation, Jesus declares his
identity: "I am he, the one who is speaking to you" (v. 26). This
formula is nothing less than the "*ego eimi*/I am who I am" that Jesus
used in identifying himself to the terrified apostles during the storm
(Matt 14:27) but now in an even more explicit form.

But just at this highly dramatic point of self-revelation and before either of them say anything else, the sacred moment is plunged into bathos by the arrival of the disciples and their reaction: they are "astonished" (shocked, amazed, or perplexed in other translations, as we noted), as they had been so often before and would still be again. Unfortunately, though, their shock appears simply to have been by the scandal of Jesus speaking with a woman. They still did not understand, and therefore they did not fully trust him. Yet still they did not have the courage of their doubts or convictions, because none of them put their concerns into words (v. 27). And on this anticlimactic note, the second movement concludes.

Recontextualization or Application

1. Do I seek authentic dialogue—or do I just like an argument?

2. Speaking the truth is more important than sinning. Do I tell the truth, or hide behind rationalizations and excuses?

3. "Believe me," says Jesus. Do I have fundamental trust in what Jesus says?

4. The woman's life will begin again with this encounter. Can my life begin again?

5. "The hour is coming and is now," says Jesus. Do I live in the present moment, or is my life governed by the past (nostalgia) or the future (wishful thinking)?

Third Movement: Discipleship—Call and Commission (vv. 28-42)

[28]Then the woman left her water jar and went back to the city. She said to the people, [29]"Come and see a man who told me everything I have ever done! He cannot be the Messiah, can he?" [30]They left the city and were on their way to him.

[31]Meanwhile the disciples were urging him, "Rabbi, eat something." [32]But he said to them, "I have food to eat that you do not know

about." ³³So the disciples said to one another, "Surely no one has brought him something to eat?" ³⁴Jesus said to them, "My food is to do the will of him who sent me and to complete his work. ³⁵Do you not say, 'Four months more, then comes the harvest'? But I tell you, look around you, and see how the fields are ripe for harvesting. ³⁶The reaper is already receiving wages and is gathering fruit for eternal life, so that sower and reaper may rejoice together. ³⁷For here the saying holds true, 'One sows and another reaps.' ³⁸I sent you to reap that for which you did not labor. Others have labored, and you have entered into their labor."

³⁹Many Samaritans from that city believed in him because of the woman's testimony, "He told me everything I have ever done." ⁴⁰So when the Samaritans came to him, they asked him to stay with them; and he stayed there two days. ⁴¹And many more believed because of his word. ⁴²They said to the woman, "It is no longer because of what you said that we believe, for we have heard for ourselves, and we know that this is truly the Savior of the world."

The third movement opens dramatically, as the woman—who came to draw water and whose life depended on it—abruptly leaves her water jar and goes back to the city. This is an act of purposefulness, not forgetfulness; and she does not go back to her own home but returns to "the city." It may be afternoon and the quiet time of day, but she is in no mood now for stealth or secrecy (which may have been part of her motivation in coming to the well at that particular time). She deliberately leaves the jar because it is now much less important than it was; and she deliberately seeks out the community because the message of Jesus concerns everyone in town.

Very suddenly, her priorities have been radically rethought and redirected. It is now she who actually calls her own people to come to Jesus, to see "a man who told me everything I have ever done!" (v. 29); something of an exaggeration, this, but clearly an indication of the profound effect Jesus has had on her in a very short time, and of her sense that he knows her as well as she knows herself. "He cannot be the Messiah, can he?" is a conventionally worded question that expects a positive answer. In other words, she is intimating, implying, that she herself believes that he is the Messiah. Now she is very close indeed to acknowledging her faith in Jesus. But the community's response at this stage is no better than halfhearted: "They left the city and were on their way to him" (v. 30) is couched in the imperfect tense, indicating here a less-than-enthusiastic, but probably curious, response—tentative rather than determined. Her testimony has done enough to pique their curiosity, but no more at this point.

While this drama is going on back in the town, the disciples (that is, the Twelve intimates of Jesus and ostensibly the exemplars of discipleship) are concerned with much more material things: food. They have themselves eaten, but they show concern for Jesus. However, while the woman has progressed from calling Jesus "Sir" to identifying him as "Messiah," they can still only muster a pedestrian "Rabbi" (teacher). They are far from coming to the faith that the woman is increasingly demonstrating. Jesus offers them a little theological lesson—which is quite lost on them, but intended by the evangelist for a later audience.

Playing on the word "food," Jesus first declares that he has food they are unaware of—which they take literally and wonder who could have brought him lunch as, evidently, they had not—and proceeds to speak about the "food" (Greek: *brōma*, meat, meal, sustenance) that is his mission of obedience to his *Abba*. But he is explicit in speaking of his own mission as one of extending and fulfilling this mission—not of bringing it to an end, as much as continuing it toward its end; others will continue it, as the woman is doing and as every disciple is called to do. At this moment, his "food" or mission is to be in Samaria on this particular day, doing non-Jewish things among non-Jewish people, while unconditionally accepting God's will in this matter. It is a lesson for each of us, a lesson of living in the present moment.

The work of mission of Jesus—as of his disciples, then and now— each day and in every place is the work of evangelizing (putting the "zing" in the Good News): that is, incarnating and disseminating the message and the promise of the realm of God, not simply in word but by changing the world and people by means of "integral evangelization"—proclamation, witness, dialogue, and liberation; or encounter, table-fellowship, footwashing and boundary-crossing (see chap. 2).

Jesus wants to radically shift the disciples' perspective. Appealing to their common sense, he says that the obvious signs on the land around them point to a harvest several months ahead: the grain has not yet produced the ears of wheat or barley, oats or millet, for it is still spring; it is not yet time. But, says Jesus, look again, and with the eyes of faith this time: the harvest is *here* and *now*. Can you not see that—even here, in Samaria, at the wrong time of the year—the grace of God is ripening the fields of the local Samaritan population so quickly that harvest time is right here! His agrarian allusion describes the normal course of events, in which the sower and the reaper are separated in time by many months, and sowers and reapers may well be different people. But in the present case, everything seems to have merged into a single event: today the woman herself will become both sower and reaper. But she was not the first, nor the last, in Samaria. John the Baptist had certainly preached there—as of course Jesus himself. And later there would be Philip (Acts 8:4-13), and perhaps even some of the Twelve themselves, or the other disciples.

This extraordinary story ends with a series of developments. First, "Many Samaritans from that city believed in him because of the woman's testimony" (v. 39). This is striking enough, given that women were regarded as unreliable witnesses, and that this woman appears to have had something of a reputation. Even some of those who later said they themselves witnessed the resurrection did not believe the women disciples who went to the tomb and then reported the news, because they could not corroborate it independently (Luke 24:22-24). This anonymous Samaritan woman is the first "Christian" missionary disciple in the New Testament. She evangelizes—brings the Good News to—her own community. Meanwhile the Twelve are far behind in their understanding of Jesus and his mission, and have completely missed the critically important interaction between

Jesus and the woman. Furthermore, members of the Samaritan community who, only moments before, had been tentative and hesitant, have now experienced something that has radically changed their attitude. Their lukewarm interest turns to true hospitality when they, Samaritans, invite a Jewish man, and a stranger, to stay—and he stays for two days. This is in stark contrast to the story of the Gerasene demoniac. On that occasion, the people "begged him to leave" because they were not ready for a conversion of heart (Mark 5:17).

In the course of those two days, many more in the community came to believe because of the evangelizing activity of Jesus. All four elements of integral evangelization are evident here: proclamation, witness, dialogue, and liberation. The latter is particularly evident in the woman's social and moral rehabilitation; she is "set free" within the community and not condemned by Jesus.

Unfortunately, the men seem to insist on having the last word, which actually makes them look rather shallow and churlishly gynophobic: "It is no longer because of what you said . . . for we have heard for ourselves" (v. 42). Although this is a totally unnecessary comment, it is informative in two ways: these people have *heard* (and we previously emphasized the importance of having ears, listening, and then internalizing and responding); but now they *know*, and they identify Jesus not only as Messiah (a more restricted term) but as "Savior of the world" (a universalizing statement that transcends all local distinctions and divisions).

At first sight, and in the judgment of many, the Samaritan woman is so very "wrong": she is the wrong ethnicity, the wrong gender, the wrong theology, the wrong lifestyle (and, say some commentators, probably menstruating, so the wrong ritual state); and yet, for Jesus, she is exactly the right person in the right place at the right time for the "God-gift" and the reception of the Good News. It can be the same for each of us.

Recontextualization or Application

1. Can I leave my "jar" behind? What is the "jar" that keeps me locked in a routine?

2. The disciples are quick to be scandalized, even by Jesus. Am I as quick to judge and to jump to unwarranted conclusions?

3. Who is this Jesus for me? Can I put words around my current understanding?

4. What, if anything, do I have to say to my own community? Dare I say it?

13

A Stranger's Gift; A Host's Revelation
(Luke 24:13-35)

Overview

This story is a long one, although not as long as the story of the woman at the well. But since it falls easily into two parts, we can treat it in two sections. By the time it is finished, we are left with multiple invitations. So instead of recontextualizing it by means of a series of questions, as in the case of the other chapters, we will identify the various invitations that we might consider in the context of our lives today.

The Gift of the Stranger (vv. 13-29)

[13]Now on that same day [of the resurrection] two of them were going to a village called Emmaus, about seven miles from Jerusalem, [14]and talking with each other about all these things that had happened. [15]While they were talking and discussing, Jesus himself came near and went with them, [16]but their eyes were kept from recognizing him. [17]And he said to them, "What are you discussing with each other while you walk along?" They stood still, looking sad. [18]Then one of them, whose name was Cleopas, answered him, "Are you the only stranger in Jerusalem who does not know the things that have taken place there in these days?" [19]He asked them, "What things?" They replied, "The things about Jesus of Nazareth, who was a prophet

mighty in deed and word before God and all the people, ²⁰and how our chief priests and leaders handed him over to be condemned to death and crucified him. ²¹But we had hoped that he was the one to redeem Israel. Yes, and besides all this, it is now the third day since these things took place. ²²Moreover, some women of our group astounded us. They were at the tomb early this morning, ²³and when they did not find his body there, they came back and told us that they had indeed seen a vision of angels who said that he was alive. ²⁴Some of those who were with us went to the tomb and found it just as the women had said; but they did not see him." ²⁵Then he said to them, "Oh, how foolish you are, and how slow of heart to believe all that the prophets have declared!" ²⁶Was it not necessary that the Messiah should suffer these things and then enter into his glory?" ²⁷Then beginning with Moses and all the prophets, he interpreted to them the things about himself in all the scriptures.

²⁸As they came near the village to which they were going, he walked ahead as if he were going on. ²⁹But they urged him strongly, saying, "Stay with us, because it is almost evening and the day is now nearly over." So he went in to stay with them.

"The Way" of Jesus leads to Jerusalem, but on the very day of the resurrection, after being given assurance that he was alive, two erstwhile disciples are actually leaving Jerusalem and heading in completely the opposite direction. Something is very wrong. Perhaps that is why the text begins with the word (omitted in the English translation), "Behold!" It is as if Luke wants to make a point that something is not right with this picture. Exactly why they were going to Emmaus is unknown, but they evidently had a plan and a specific destination, though they had lost their nerve, their faith, and their true sense of direction. It is possible that they were a married couple, since the man was named but not the woman (a conventional mode of identification). But it is most unlikely that this Cleopas (v. 18) was the same person as the Clopas, husband of a woman called Mary who stood at the foot of the cross (John 19:25). That particular Mary would hardly be leaving Jerusalem if she had been so faithful at the cross; so the Cleopas in our story must be a different person from the Clopas in John's gospel. Also, this Cleopas will refer to "some women of our group," and if Mary the wife of Cleopas was one of them, then she is not the person Jesus meets on the road to Emmaus. So we are left with the unlikely possibility that the travelers are two men and, the more likely one, that they are a married couple, the husband being a man called Cleopas and the wife being unnamed.

What we do know is that they were engaged in serious discussion about the events of the previous three days, when Jesus appeared. Evidently he had gone *out of his way* in an exceptional fashion: this is, after all, the day of the resurrection. But it also shows very well just what Jesus will do to call and commission disciples. So he had caught up with them and now "went with them" (v. 15). The verb indicates that he accompanied them, and the root of the word ac-company is —*pan*, meaning bread: a com*pan*ion or a person who accom*pan*ies another is a "bread-sharer," and that will prove to be a very significant fact in this story.

"But their eyes were kept from recognizing him" (v. 16) is in the passive voice (no subject is specified) and it looks like another example of a *divine passive* like the ones we saw in the case of the bent-over woman (chap. 8), which always indicate that God is the subject or agent of the sentence. But since this is the risen Christ and not a resuscitated corpse, we have no idea of Jesus' physical appearance. But the documentary evidence shows that nobody recognized the risen Christ by his features, only by his voice; so in effect he was unrecognizable. For this reason alone, their eyes were kept from recognizing him.

Jesus adopts an unusual approach to the travelers. First, he comes upon them while they are deep in conversation and attaches himself to them; then he asks what they are talking about. If this happened to us, we would probably be at first rather uncomfortable and then indignant, thinking: What does our conversation have to do with you? But for some reason they do not take offense, even when he insults them a little later on; evidently there is something compelling about this interloper. But their immediate reaction to his question is that "they stood still, looking sad" (v. 17); they have literally nothing to say for themselves and are evidently quite dispirited (and dis-Spirited). Cleopas, the spokesperson, finally indicates that what they are discussing is the news of the hour and common knowledge to anyone in Jerusalem. And he identifies Jesus as a "stranger"—of whom there would be hundreds, even thousands, in Jerusalem at the time. But even the strangers should know what had happened. Yet very disingenuously Jesus asks, "What things?" And at that point the travelers' tale pours out in an unending stream. But the fact that Jesus is identified as—or assumed to be—a stranger, is significant. This is one of only two occasions in the New Testament where Jesus is so identified. The other is in Matthew 25:35-45, where Jesus speaks of the time when "the Son of Man comes in his glory" at the end time. He will identify himself as a stranger, and judge people according to their treatment of the strangers they encounter in the course of their life. Jesus says explicitly, "I was a stranger." Here, however, it is the travelers who identify Jesus as a stranger, but Jesus does not demur: he wants to be seen as a stranger. The question will then be, how will they treat this stranger?

Once Cleopas or his companion begins to speak, there is simply no stopping them. They identify Jesus as a mighty prophet, and tell how he came to be crucified. But then they betray themselves with the statement, "But we had hoped that he was the one to redeem Israel" (v. 21), that is, the one who would restore the people's fortunes by delivering them from their current oppression. But for a disciple, a follower of Christ, hope can never become a thing of the past: hope is a nonnegotiable, a sign of commitment. Hope is faith, but in the future mode: today we live in and by faith, and tomorrow we will continue to do so. Hope is today's faith pledged for tomorrow and all our tomorrows. But we must not wait until tomorrow before we commit ourselves to hope, for our commitment is now—and forever. To say "we had hoped," therefore, is to admit that we no longer hope; and those who no longer have hope are on the edge of despair—the absence of hope. These travelers are in a bad way and far from the Way of Jesus at this point.

But they are not finished. Now they proceed to tell Jesus that they have received serious circumstantial evidence that Jesus is alive: they have been "astounded" (a word that recurs so frequently that it might be part of the job description—or the default position—of a disciple) by reports from the women who went to the tomb, and from the angels they claimed to have seen. But women's testimony was regarded as unreliable in law, and despite being astounded, *and* having the women's testimony corroborated by their own associates ("some of those who were with us," v. 24), still they do not believe.[1] Evidently, then, mere miracles do not make faith; it is faith that makes miracles. And Jesus tells them they are foolish and slow—literally, "mindless," "lacking a mind," and "doltish" or "slow-minded" (v. 25). Yet even at this, they do not seem to take offense! He then rehearses all the events that led to his crucifixion, adding that it was "needful" for these things to happen (v. 27). In other words, he is intimating that God's hand, the hand of Divine Providence, was always guiding the outcome of events.

By now they have reached Emmaus. And Jesus, the stranger, the gentle interloper, does exactly what protocol demands: he does not presume anything, and simply attempts to proceed on his way. But, surprisingly, given their situation and preoccupation, the travelers still manage to treat Jesus with the hospitality due to a stranger, and they invite him to dine with them. In fact they urge him, on the grounds that it is getting toward dusk, and he should not be out in the dark. The real reason is, of course, that they have been captivated and reinvigorated by him, and they do not want to lose him. And Jesus gently acquiesces.

Recontextualization or Application

1. Where am I going? Am I headed in the right direction? Do I need a change of course?

2. "Their eyes were kept from recognizing him." How aware and perceptive am I of the ways in which the Christ appears to me daily in disguise?

3. Do I still hope, or have I given up? How might my hope be revived?

4. Am I skeptical of other people's experience or knowledge? Do I always want to see for myself before I make a commitment?

5. When did I last show real hospitality to a stranger?

The Revelation of the Host (vv. 30-35)

> [30]When he was at the table with them, he took bread, blessed and broke it, and gave it to them. [31]Then their eyes were opened, and they recognized him; and he vanished from their sight. [32]They said to each other, "Were not our hearts burning within us while he was talking to us on the road, while he was opening the scriptures to us?" [33]That same hour they got up and returned to Jerusalem; and they found the eleven and their companions gathered together. [34]They were saying, "The Lord has risen indeed, and he has appeared to Simon!" [35]Then they told what had happened on the road, and how he had been made known to them in the breaking of the bread.

From this point on, there is a radical shift in the relationship between Jesus and his hosts, for it is he, and not they, who now takes on the role of the host: *he* took the bread; *he* blessed and broke it; and *he* gave it to them. For the greater part of the history of the church, the fourfold action of Jesus in this story—taking, blessing, breaking, and giving—has been the structural core of the Eucharist we celebrate today. Together with the threefold action over the cup—taking, blessing, giving—this constitutes the sevenfold eucharistic action. Evidently the church has understood the action of Jesus at the table in Emmaus to be another "type" or foreshadowing of the Eucharist. The similarity between Emmaus and our contemporary Eucharist does not end there. Immediately after Jesus took, blessed, broke, and shared the bread, the text says, "Then their eyes were opened, and they recognized him, and he vanished from their sight" (v. 31). First, "their eyes were opened" is yet another *divine passive* indicating the direct act of God. So God opened their already-open eyes even more widely so that they could see what they previously failed to see. And now they recognize Jesus in the very moment of his physical disappearance. The Greek verb indicates that previous knowledge is now being employed in such a way that the person they now recognize as Jesus was the person they had previously seen and known, but had not realized that fact until this moment. This is the same Jesus of Nazareth, although unrecognizable as the risen Christ until now. But in this moment they are enlightened and able to identify the Jesus they previously knew, with the risen Christ sitting before them. But precisely at that moment, "He vanished from their sight" (v. 31).

Here we have a wonderful depiction of what the church has tried to explain for centuries: the Real Presence of Christ. But since it is a mystery, it cannot be comprehensively explained, only described approximately and accepted in faith. We believe that Jesus is "really present" in the Eucharist. But this is not a crude physical presence; it is a sacramental presence. Not a mere symbol and no longer the risen and glorified body of the crucified one, Jesus is nevertheless, in his absence, really, truly present in the Eucharist, but sacramentally so.

A sacrament is a real and palpable sign that points to something beyond, and it has three characteristics. First, an authentic sign must point in the right direction. Second, it must contain correct information. And, third, it must be legible. A sign that says "Paris, 4,000 miles" does not point to itself but to a distant reality. But if it is not pointing in the right direction it is a countersign or a false sign. And if the name or the distance is illegible, the sign is virtually useless. So it is with a sacrament. And what is happening at that table in Emmaus? Jesus is really, truly present with them—and then he vanishes in his physical, bodily being. And yet he is still there, still present, in the bread they hold in their trembling hands, in those trembling hands themselves, in the retinas of their eyes that hold his image, in their hearts still burning from the encounter, and in their memories. He is both really present and yet has vanished physically from their sight. It is surely a mystery, but they know, with utter conviction, that it is true.

There is a moment when no words are spoken because there are simply no adequate words to express their experience. Each knew the other had recognized him; they knew that he was really there; and they knew that he had both vanished yet was present. And then they began to speak, to articulate their inchoate thoughts, to begin to make sense of the strange and confusing—yet uplifting and restorative—experience of the previous hours. Now they discover that they both had the same feelings of elation and newly burning hope as they were "accompanied" by the one who broke the bread and showed them the Way they had failed to follow but abandoned in hopelessness. So without delay—having told Jesus it was too late to be out in the dark—they retraced their steps, but at a much quicker pace now. The eleven were also sharing a meal with their companions, presumably the faithful women who had been first at the tomb that morning, and becoming increasingly convinced that something unprecedented had really happened: Jesus had risen as he said!

The dis-Spirited (but now inspired) disciples have the last word in this extraordinary story: they retell their own story, understanding it better each time they repeat it, witnessing to the eleven that Jesus had accompanied them on the way, had led the way, and had reoriented them to the Way of Jesus, from which they would now never deviate. They were able to witness that all this had been done through the power of God, but the full revelation had been concentrated in that consecrated moment when they no longer simply *knew about* Jesus. Now they *actually knew* him, intimately. And they would never forget: it had happened in the taking, blessing, breaking and sharing of the bread.

Recontextualization or Application

A Sixfold Call from Jesus

1. A call to "resurrection faith": What is my personal commitment to the risen Christ, alive among us today?

2. A call to reinterpret my life: To what incompletions must I return? What wounds must I revisit?

3. A call to remember when my heart was burning: When was my faith and zeal strong?

4. A call to look for Jesus: How do I see Jesus at the table? In com-*pan*-ions? In hospitality? In the stranger? In the Eucharist?

5. A call to see and to recognize how God meets me in my daily journeys: In what ways is God recognizable and really present?

6. A call to live my life of faith more intentionally: How may I stay close to Jesus? How may I be a messenger—and evangelizer—of the Good News?

14

A Faithful Doubter
(John 20:24-29)

²⁴But Thomas (who was called the Twin), one of the twelve, was not with them when Jesus came. ²⁵So the other disciples told him, "We have seen the Lord." But he said to them, "Unless I see the mark of the nails in his hands, and put my finger in the mark of the nails and my hand in his side, I will not believe."

²⁶A week later his disciples were again in the house, and Thomas was with them. Although the doors were shut Jesus came and stood among them and said, "Peace be with you." ²⁷Then he said to Thomas, "Put your finger here and see my hands. Reach out your hand and put it in my side. Do not doubt but believe." ²⁸Thomas answered him, "My Lord and my God!" ²⁹Jesus said to him, "Have you believed because you have seen me? Blessed are those who have not seen and yet have come to believe."

Thomas seems rather strange, or odd, at times. Perhaps his name gives us a hint that he was different. In this story he is identified as "the Twin," but since we have absolutely no information about the other twin, it seems legitimate to ask why he was so named if that fact is effectively irrelevant. But the Greek might help us here, for the word *didymus* not only means "twin," but, presumably by association, also means "testicle." If this was a nickname, it may also be a hint that Thomas was somehow different, somehow lacking, as he apparently "lacked" his other twin. We will never know. The first indication that he was different, however, is John's observation that "he was not with them" (v. 24) when Jesus came on the evening of the day of resurrection and showed himself to the twelve-minus-two (vv. 19-23): for Judas was not with them either. In the case of Judas, we do know his fate, sadly. But where on earth was Thomas on the day of the resurrection? In a previous verse we read that the apostles were huddled together for company behind locked doors "for fear of the Jews" (v. 19) in their initial fear and confusion after the crucifixion. Yet Thomas has somehow already disappeared.

If we trace his interventions prior to that day, we find him in the company of Jesus when Jesus announces that his friend Lazarus is dead, and then expresses his intention to go to Lazarus, and to Martha and Mary, "so that you may believe." Thomas responds—petulantly, truculently, or fatalistically, we do not know—"Let us also go, so that we may die with him" (John 11:15-16): hardly an indication that he believes. It sounds as though he has already given up. Later, during the Last Supper, Jesus again calls the apostles to believe in him, and says that he is leaving but he will return—something he had already told them quite explicitly (Mark 10:23-45). But Thomas is the first responder, saying, "Lord, we do not know where you are going. How can we know the way?" Jesus says, "I am the way" (John 14:5-6). Between that interaction and the one we are considering here, Thomas is silent and absent, including (according to John's account) on the day of the resurrection itself. Curiously, though, Luke says that "the eleven" were all together (Luke 24:34) when the two travelers returned from Emmaus late at night. But John's story of Thomas's transformation from skeptic or doubter to believer requires his absence on the occasion of Jesus' post-resurrection appearance.

Some time later, the rest of the apostles tell him of their experience with the risen Lord (vv. 24-25). But Thomas flatly refuses to believe their unanimous testimony. Some people are like that, and Thomas appears to be one of them: different and expecting to be treated as a special case. And, judging by his outburst, he is also angry and deeply hurt, for twice he refers to Jesus not by name but only as "he," in the third person. This is precisely the reaction of someone who feels wounded and talks about his or her putative offender to a third party but without dignifying that person by uttering his or her name. To refer to someone we know, in anger, as "he" (or "she") effectively reduces the friend to the status of enemy, at least temporarily. Thomas is also issuing an ultimatum to Jesus; soon, like Peter, he will regret it bitterly. Like a temperamental child or adolescent he makes an absolute and universal statement, metaphorically stamping his foot: "I will not believe," he says, unless the precise terms of his ultimatum are met.

Another week passes after his outburst, and now, equally unexplained, Thomas is with the rest of the apostles, never imagining that Jesus would appear. Luke tells us that the doors were shut, indicating that the apostles had still not come to terms with the fact of the risen Christ. Suddenly Jesus is really present among them, despite the locked doors. And the first words he utters are "Peace be with you!" (plural). This is what is called a "performative utterance": the words actually bring about the outcome; they generate the action they speak of. When a person is baptized, the words "I baptize you" are performative: as they are uttered and the action performed, so the person is actually baptized. "I now declare you husband and wife" or "I launch this ship" are also performatives (assuming the ship actually moves, otherwise they are a failed performative and acutely embarrassing). So Jesus is not at all saying the equivalent of "Have a nice day," or offering a simple conventional greeting. He is doing something very profound.

Everyone in that room is struggling to come to terms with the recent events. They are not at peace with themselves, nor with each other—particularly the petulant and absent Thomas. The air must be electric with their mistrust and self-recriminations. Yet Jesus does not upbraid them. He brings his peace into that room and into the heart and soul of each person there. The peace of which he talks is the peace the world cannot give because the world does not know it (cf. John 14:27). This is another "God-gift": the gift *is* God, the God of peace. Consequently, if people have this gift, it resides at the very deepest part of their being, and even the turmoil on the surface and in their daily lives cannot destroy it. This peace is rather like the stillness in the deepest parts of the ocean that hurricanes and typhoons on the surface cannot touch. And this is the gratuitous gift Jesus offers his disciples.

And then he turns to Thomas, who at this point must already be distinctly uncomfortable before the palpable presence of Jesus, not to mention the fact that he is surrounded by the very people before whom he melodramatically declared the terms of his ultimatum. But Jesus has just brought peace upon the community and now addresses him directly. The room is still, and no one moves, but every eye is upon Thomas.

This is no judgmental Jesus, and there are no harsh words. This is the teacher addressing one of the learners who still has so much to learn. But it is the gentle Jesus, not some strict and demanding teacher; this is the Jesus not of "religion" and rules that constrict, but of "revelation" and possibilities that liberate. This is the Jesus who forgives seventy times seven, and always goes beyond and reaches out to embrace the bruised and wounded—even when they lash out at those who try to help. But this is no codependent Jesus, either, making it too easy for Thomas to continue his childish pouting. Jesus is now about to do exactly what Thomas had petulantly demanded, and let Thomas feel the consequences. This must be the longest moment of Thomas's life—an excruciating, heart-stopping moment, so painful that it brings him, almost literally, to his knees. Thomas, of course, had made impossible stipulations: that he be allowed to put his finger in the obscenely mutilated hands of Jesus, and, even more grossly intrusive, to put his hand in the awful, gaping puncture wound in his side. But making eye contact that Thomas, now mesmerized, could not avoid, Jesus invites Thomas to do precisely what he had so outrageously demanded. And while urging Thomas to reach out his hand, Jesus invites him also to believe and have no doubts at all that this really is the risen Jesus standing before him.

There is no reason for us to think that Thomas actually raised his hand, and every reason to think he did not raise his voice. But in a whisper, scarcely audible, and full of as much deep shame as it was of fragile faith, he heard the words tumbling from his bone-dry mouth: "My Lord and my God!" (v. 28). It is the most concise and complete, the most personal and faith-filled utterance in the whole of the New Testament. There is no air left in Thomas's lungs and no movement in that room—only breathless stillness. And Jesus speaks. "Thomas," he says with compassion yet great sadness and disappointment, "Have you believed [only] because you have seen me?" (v. 29).

Yes, indeed, Thomas has come to believe because now he has seen with his own eyes what his mind was unable to imagine and would not let him see. Yes, Thomas has come to faith the long way around, by the slow and winding road, resisting "the Way" that Jesus himself had been taking, the way he had shown Thomas and the others these many months. Yes, Thomas, at last, has come to faith, tentatively and by degrees, not like blind Bartimaeus who called him "*Rabboni, my teacher*"; not like the bent-over woman who was so faithfully present and profoundly "there" in the synagogue; not like the anonymous and deeply faith-filled woman who anointed Jesus; and not like Jairus who believed that God was working through the ministry of Jesus, or the bleeding woman who believed he could heal her; not even like the Samaritan woman who had come to faith in a single afternoon and then become a missionary disciple, nor like the disciples on the road to Emmaus who admitted they "had hoped" but had given up, and yet returned to Jerusalem with speed and conviction. But now Thomas too was *there*, trembling before Jesus and pouring out his newfound faith.

In that heart-stopping moment, he must have understood at last what his life was all about. In that lung-bursting instant, he must have known for certain who Jesus really was. In those long and frightening seconds when Jesus spoke, he must have received the enlightenment of grace and the grace of enlightenment. Maybe that is why Thomas is such a favorite with so many of us who doubt, struggle, and try to persevere and remain *there*. We are just like him. We too come to faith, by the low, slow road, but by God's grace we do come to know the Way and try to follow it, and to stay close to the one who blazes the trail, clears the way, and goes before us to show us how we are to follow him.

Recontextualization or Application

1. Am I really as self-assured as I sometimes appear, like Thomas?

2. What makes me so angry, frightened, petulant, childish, and demanding?

3. Do I miss some of life's critically important events because I am not there?

4. Which is stronger in my life—doubt or trust?

Notes

Introduction

[1] I will use "the Way" with a capital letter when drawing attention not simply to a path, a road, or a way to a place, but specifically to "the Way" of Jesus as a reference to Christian discipleship itself. This is not a matter of finding our own way to Jesus, but of encountering or being called by Jesus and thereby discovering his own Way—to Jerusalem, to crucifixion, and to resurrection—which every disciple is called to follow.

[2] Dietrich Bonhoeffer, *The Cost of Discipleship* (New York: Simon & Schuster, 1995), 38.

[3] There is a helpful description of this kind of conversation-by-invitation in Ernesto Cardenal, *The Gospel in Solentiname*, 4 vols. (Maryknoll, NY: Orbis, 1976): A small faith-sharing community of simple people, mostly with little formal education but vibrant and resilient faith, came together with the gentle leadership of their pastor. Their insights and their cultural context are inspiring and illuminating. Eric H. F. Law proposes this kind of approach, which he calls "Mutual Invitation"; well worth referring to, it can be found in his *The Wolf Shall Dwell with the Lamb: A Spirituality for Leadership in a Multicultural Community* (St. Louis, MO: Chalice Press, 1993), 79–88.

Chapter 1

[1] Blase Cupich, "Our Place in the Unfolding Story," Reflection, *Give Us This Day* 5, no. 5 (May 2015): 323.

Chapter 2

[1] Robert Karris, *Eating Your Way Through Luke's Gospel* (Collegeville, MN: Liturgical Press, 2006).

[2] Pope Francis, *Evangelii Gaudium* (The Joy of the Gospel), apostolic exhortation, November 24, 2013.

Chapter 3

[1] As the Gospel of John concludes, "But there are also many other things that Jesus did; if every one of them were written down, I suppose that the world itself could not contain the books that would be written" (John 21:25).

[2] For an extended, exciting, and scholarly treatment, see John P. Meier, *A Marginal Jew: Rethinking the Historical Jesus*, vol. III (New York: Doubleday, 1991), 50–54, 70–80.

[3] Austin Flannery, ed., *Vatican Council II: Constitutions, Decrees, Declarations; The Basic Sixteen Documents* (Collegeville, MN: Liturgical Press, 2014).

[4] There are dozens of references to "the Way" in the New Testament. Disciples of the Pharisees say, "Teacher, we know that you are sincere, and teach *the way* of God in accordance with the truth" (Matt 22:16); "Thomas said, . . . 'How can we know *the way*?' Jesus said to him, 'I am *the way*'" (John 14:4-6). Also Acts 9:2; 18:25-26; 19:19, 24; 22:4; 24:22; and many more.

[5] See Bruce M. Metzger and Michael D. Coogan, eds., *The Oxford Companion to the Bible* (New York: Oxford University Press, 1993), 357.

[6] Meier, *A Marginal Jew*, 53.

[7] In Romans 16, Paul speaks of other apostles, some of whom he says are greater than himself. They include the women, Junia(s), and Prisca. He also speaks polemically and even pejoratively about unnamed others whom he calls "these super-apostles" (2 Cor 11:5).

Chapter 4

[1] Vladimir Kharlamov, ed., *Theosis: Deification in Christian Tradition* (Eugene, OR: Pickwick Publications, 2011). And see Thomas Aquinas, *Summa Theologica*, III, q. I, a. 3 for a fuller discussion.

[2] Athanasius, "On the Incarnation of the Word," trans. John Behr (Yonkers, NY: St. Vladimir's Seminary Press, 2011), 167.

[3] Irenaeus, *Adversus Haereses*, 3. 10. 2, in *Patrologia Cursus Completus, Series Graeca*, PG 7.873 (Migne, ed.).

[4] *Catechism of the Catholic Church*, 2nd ed. (United States Catholic Conference—Libreria Editrice Vaticana, 1997), 460, 1129, 1265, 1812, and 1988.

[5] This is the topic of chapter 14.

[6] The only woman actually identified as *mathētria* is Tabitha or Dorcas, in Acts 9:36, so Luke does acknowledge women disciples, though not in his gospel.

[7] Dietrich Bonhoeffer, *The Cost of Discipleship* (New York: Simon & Schuster, 1995), 59.

Chapter 5

[1] For a masterful development of this theme, see Vincent J. Donovan, *The Church in the Midst of Creation* (Maryknoll, NY: Orbis, 1989), 84–90.

[2] At the end of each chapter in part 2 there are suggestions for personal reflection. Many questions could be generated from a careful reading of the text in order to be posed as a test to each of us in our current circumstances. See the end of chapter 4 for the rationale.

Chapter 6

[1] Bruce Chilton, in *The Oxford Companion to the Bible*, ed. Bruce M. Metzger and Michael D. Coogan, 408–9 (New York: Oxford University Press, 1993).

Chapter 7

[1] This is not sexist language: only men had honor. Women were expected to increase the honor of their menfolk by their virtuous behavior. The "problem" with women is that they could also contribute to their men's shame by their bad behavior—which accounts for the "honor killings" in our day that are done by men to forestall their women's scandalous and therefore shameful (to the men) actions, such as deciding whom to marry without male approval.

Chapter 8

[1] Luke Timothy Johnson, *The Gospel of Luke*, Sacra Pagina series, ed. Daniel J. Harrington (Collegeville, MN: Liturgical Press, 1991), 212.

[2] For proclamation, witness, dialogue, and liberation—four constitutive components of the ministry of Jesus—see chapter 2.

[3] Skeletal evidence puts a man's life expectancy at only 29 years, and a woman's even less.

[4] A distinction should be made here between the *social death* of the woman and the rules of religious purity discussed in chap. 2 (pp. 35–36 and elsewhere in these stories). There is a danger that Christians can reveal deep prejudice and ignorance about Jewish belief and practice. Amy-Jill Levine is a Jewish scholar of the New Testament whose writings—especially *The Misunderstood Jew: The Church and the Scandal of the Jewish Jesus* (San Francisco: HarperOne, 2007), 173–80—provide an important corrective. Most helpfully, Professor

Levine clarifies distinctions between legal-religious prescriptions and actual behaviors (whether observant or deviant), the latter of which are, of course, not always in strict conformity with the former.

⁵ Daniel O'Leary, "And Did Those Feet . . . ," *The Tablet* (August 18, 2012): 8. It was particularly sad and ironic that shortly after I read this piece, an announcement from the Congregation for Divine Worship announced that liturgical law "does not foresee the use of dance or drama [within Mass] unless particular legislation has been enacted by the Bishop's Conference" (*Catholic Herald*, London, UK [October 12, 2012]: 4).

⁶ In none of the gospels is any woman identified specifically as a disciple. Only in Acts 9:36 does Luke name Tabitha, or Dorcas, as a disciple, using the feminine of the word *mathētēs*, which is *mathētria*.

Chapter 9

¹ The only two criteria for the designation "apostle" were to have been with Jesus from the beginning and to have been a witness to the resurrection. Saint Paul and those he calls "apostles" do not fulfill either or both, but Mary Magdalene certainly fulfills the latter, if not the former. Sadly she is still too often portrayed as a sinner and with an alabaster jar nearby, thus misidentifying her again.

² Mark does not explicitly say that the Twelve were at the house of Simon the leper, placing this meal a day prior to the "Last Supper" and implying that Judas, at least, was there (Mark 14:10). Matthew's narrative follows that of Mark, but he places Jesus' prediction of Judas's betrayal at the Last Supper itself (Matt 26:21-25). Luke gives it an entirely different context and only refers to Judas's betrayal obliquely (Luke 22:22). John does not refer to it.

³ Robert Karris, *Eating Your Way Through Luke's Gospel* (Collegeville, MN: Liturgical Press, 2006) is a splendidly accessible book on this topic.

⁴ This verb is the same as the one expressing Jesus' indignation; the verb for "they scolded her" is even more violent, translated as to "snort with anger."

⁵ She is not a slave and therefore not operating under duress. She is acting freely and courageously: the act of a *diakonos* (assistant) rather than of a *doulos* (slave).

⁶ See footnote 6, chapter 4.

⁷ Interestingly these words are not found in Mark's gospel—nor in Matthew or John, and only once (over the bread) in Luke. It is Paul, claiming to have received this tradition "from the Lord," who repeats these words over both the bread and the wine (1 Cor 11:23-25).

⁸ Mark's account, being the prelude to the passion narrative, is indeed read on the first Sunday of Passiontide ("Palm Sunday"). But by the time that long narrative is concluded 15–20 minutes later, she is effectively forgotten and virtually never preached on. The only other occasion Mark's story *is* told is on a weekday in Ordinary Time when few people gather and fewer homilies are preached.

Chapter 10

¹ Contemplation, as we saw (chap. 2, fig. 2), is the dynamo that energizes the evangelizing mission and ministry of Jesus—and every disciple needs to emulate Jesus in this matter.

² Three stages of discipleship: call/encounter, disturbance/displacement, sending/co-missioning are identified in chapter 4.

³ "And they were utterly astounded, for they did not understand about the loaves, but their hearts were hardened" (Mark 6:51-52).

Chapter 11

¹ In Matthew (8:28), Gadarenes. The actual location is disputed by scholars, but is of no significance for this story, except to note that the people of that place had begged Jesus to leave (Matt 8:34), in contrast to the approaches of the two protagonists in this story.

² A reminder that this word *ochlos*, "crowd," is a generic term that includes the rank and file, the riffraff, the motley, insignificant or marginal people so sought out and privileged by Jesus.

³ Leviticus 15:19, 25. The latter verse, which relates to a chronic condition, declares that "all the days of the discharge [a woman] shall continue in uncleanness." The chapter continues with strict instructions for the woman and for anyone who encounters her; and v. 31 declares that these measures are so that the people of Israel will be effectively separated from their uncleanness. Contrary to popular opinion, however, the Law (Lev 15:25-30) does *not* state that a woman suffering from a discharge is guilty of ritual impurity if she touches someone. See Amy-Jill Levine, *The Misunderstood Jew*, 174.

⁴ Illnesses contracted in the hospital or in the course of treatment from a physician are called iatrogenic diseases: actually caused by bad diagnosis, treatment, or surroundings.

⁵ "[King] Asa was diseased in his feet, and his disease became severe; yet even in his disease he did not seek the LORD, but sought help from physicians" (2 Chr 16:12).

⁶ The verb in the last verse of the story of the woman taken in adultery, "Go, and *do not miss the mark* again," can be spoken most effectively if Jesus has his arm around her shoulder and is pointing to an imaginary mark, her future target.

⁷ For an elaboration, see Craig Blomberg, *Contagious Holiness: Jesus' Meals with Sinners*, New Studies in Biblical Theology, ed. D. A. Carson (Downers Grove, IL: InterVarsity Press, 2005).

⁸ *Exousia*, "power," in Greek, has its roots in the verb "to be," literally "out (of) being" or "outpouring."

⁹ The same term used for the bent woman (chap. 8) and the woman who anoints Jesus (chap. 9).

Chapter 12

¹ See Bruce M. Metzger and Michael D. Coogan, eds., "Samaritans," in *The Oxford Companion to the Bible* (New York: Oxford University Press, 1993), 671–73.

² See explanation of social status as marked by the position of a person's head relative to others, in chapter 9.

Chapter 13

¹ We saw (chap. 12) that the men of Sychar, the Samaritan town, claimed that they believed Jesus, no longer because of the woman's testimony, but because they had seen and heard for themselves (John 4:42).

Scripture Index

20:25	56	18:25-26	156n4	15:5, 7	47
21:15-17	110	19:19, 24	156n4		
		22:4	156n4	**2 Corinthians**	
Acts		24:22	156n4	11:5	156n7
1:8	19–20				
3:6-8	94	**Romans**		**Ephesians**	
8:4-13	137	16	156n7	2:13-14	36
9:2	156n4				
9:36	156n6,	**1 Corinthians**		**Hebrews**	
	158n6	11:23-25	158n7	2:16-17	53